GW01339434

Jonathan Couch's
CORNISH BIRDS

Edited by

R. D. PENHALLURICK

MMIII

Polperro Heritage Press

© Polperro Heritage Press 2003

All rights reserved. No part of this publication may be reproduced or transmitted in any form or by any means, electronic or mechanical, including photocopying, recording, or any information storage and retrieval system, without prior permission in writing from the publisher.

ISBN 0-9530012-8-8

Published by
Polperro Heritage Press
Clifton-upon-Teme
Worcestershire WR6 6EN
polperro.press@virgin.net

Printed by Orphans Press
Leominster HR6 8JT
United Kingdom

CONTENTS

Acknowledgements 4

Introduction 5

Abbreviations 34

Catalogue of Cornish Birds 35

Supplement 155

Select Bibliography 181

Index of current English names of birds 184

ACKNOWLEDGEMENTS

Firstly I owe my sincere thanks to the Council of the Royal Institution of Cornwall for a substantial grant towards the publication of this book and for permission to make full use of the extensive collection of Couch material in the Royal Cornwall Museum, and secondly to the Trustees of the Sir Arthur Quiller Couch Memorial Fund for their grant towards the cost of research.

Individuals and organisations who also deserve my thanks are Angela Broome, librarian at the R.I.C., The National Trust's Cornwall Regional Office for permission to reproduce the early portrait of E.H. Rodd, and Philip Correll, a former resident of Polperro, who enlightened me on some obscure local place-names. H. L. Douch, retired Curator at the R.I. C., Rex Hall and Cedric Appleby have all over the years supplied relevant 19th century newspaper references to birds chanced upon in the course of their own researches.

Others who have supplied photocopies of material published or in manuscript, are Stella M. Turk of Camborne, Todd Gray of Exeter University, June Holmes of the Hancock Museum, Newcastle-upon-Tyne, staff at The Linnean Society of London, The Natural History Museum, London, and its sub-department of Ornithology at Tring, and the Museum of Costume at Bath.

Finally I thank my wife Pat for her eagle-eyed proof-reading and for transposing the output of my Acorn computer into Word capable of being read by most of those "high-speed morons". Dryden observed that "Errors like straws, upon the surface flow". Any errors of fact that remain flow directly from me.

R.D.P.

INTRODUCTION

Cornwall. Situated at the extremity of the Kingdom, and projecting into the depths of the Atlantic, its position, climate and mineralogical structure combine to assign it a distinguished place in natural history above most other Counties of England.

Jonathan Couch, 1838, *A Cornish Fauna*, p. v.

Dr Jonathan Couch

(15 iii 1789 - 13 iv 1870)

A BRIEF BIOGRAPHY OF JONATHAN COUCH

A good "Sketch" is given by Thomas Quiller Couch in his late father's *The History of Polperro* (Truro 1871, pp. 1-27), and includes a Bibliography of his published works. Much of this was derived from Jonathan's MS "Memorials of the family of Couch" which has been transcribed and edited by Alwyne Wheeler (*Journal of the Royal Institution of Cornwall*, 1983, pp. 92-145). Bertha Couch also published a *Life of Jonathan Couch of Polperro* in 1895 for "the many tourists who now visit that spot" and for those familiar with his writings. For its literary skill, nothing is more readable than *Memories & Opinions. An Unfinished Autobiography* by "Q", Sir Arthur Quiller Couch (1944, Cambridge University Press), Jonathan's grandson. "Q" met him only once in person on "a filial visit to which I was taken at the age of four or thereabouts ... Though actually of moderate height, he seemed to me incredibly tall, and taller yet when he laid a hand on my head and solemnly blessed me". Jonathan, he observed, was "A proud man, stiff in his Methodist ancestry, he strode his domain as its unchallengeable great man, in top-hat, high white stock, long black coat, and until past middle age, black breeches and silver-buckled shoes — a costume which forfeited no dignity as he would sit, after his wont, on an inverted fish-basket by the quay, with brush and paintbox ready and the eye of an osprey on the nets, should perchance they discharge something rare, however minute". The old doctor in "Q"s *Nicky-Nan, Reservist*, set in the first world war, who wrote a *History of Polpier* is none other than a reincarnation of Jonathan, a theme developed by Denys W. Tucker in "A Cornish Ichthyologist in fact and fiction: 'Q' on his grandfather Jonathan Couch" (*J. Soc. Bibliography of Natural History*, 1955, Vol. 3, Pt. 3, 137-151).

Couch never lost his devout Christian faith. The memorial in Polperro's Methodist Church proclaims "The deep piety which marked his labours and his preaching here permeated also his devoted service to his fellow men, and to learning, and was reflected in his many writings on natural history". What he made of Darwin's *On the Origin of Species* (1859), or even if he read it, is not known. If he did, the contents did not trouble his view that God was the supreme creator of all things. The Preface to his *British Fishes* contains a paragraph developing Linnaeus' statement about "Argument from Design", and the title-page a line from Psalm 111 that praises the glorious works of God. During his stay with Yarrell in 1849 he twice dined with Professor Richard Owen (1804-1892), anatomist and arch-believer in "the immutability of species". Couch found him "to be an open hearted man, free to communicate, and without the least appearance of assumption". This was a far cry from the feelings of many contemporaries, and Darwin himself was soon to turn with great effect Owen's own evidence to support the new "theory of evolution by means of natural selection" that sounded the death knell of Owen's scientific importance. Couch certainly believed that not everything was created by God merely for the benefit of mankind, but rather that man alone of the animals is capable of comprehending the complexities of Nature and has a duty to do so. He would have agreed with Alexander Pope who wrote:

> Has God, thou fool! work'd solely for thy good,
>
> Thy joy, thy pastime, thy attire, thy food? ...
>
> Is it for thee the lark ascends and sings?
>
> Joy tunes his voice, joy elevates his wings.
>
> Is it for thee the linnet pours his throat?
>
> Loves of his own and raptures swell the note.
>
> *Essay on Man*

Couch's own poetic words written three years before his death tell as much and the reasons for his devotion to his native village:

> 'Twas filial duty that fixed me here:
>
> To soothe a father's wish with heart sincere.
>
> An aged mother next my cares engage:
>
> To watch her comforts in extreme age.
>
> Then over all a providence presides,
>
> That snatched my joys away, and yet provides
>
> Successive comforts still to calm the breast,
>
> And bid the wandering wishes sink to rest.
>
> To vacant hours He offers Nature's stores—
>
> Abounding sea born race,
>
> Unknown the larger portion, find a place
>
> In diligent enquiry: 'till at last
>
> They fill the vacant hour, not idly pass'd.
>
> In all his works I trace the hand of God,
>
> Nor more in living Nature than the rod
>
> Of his chastening hand; but more than these,
>
> His care has fixed my dwelling, where to please
>
> My kind preserver is my highest bliss:
>
> And what a high reward I find in this!

Jonathan, the only son of Richard and Philippa Couch, was born in a cottage on the Talland side of Polperro on 15 March 1789. The house where he resided throughout his adult life, still known as Couch's House, is a different dwelling in the centre of the village behind the quay. His education began at the local dame school and one of his prized possessions was a horn book purchased later in life, when such things had become very rare, similar to, but older than the one he had used when learning to read and write. At eight he moved to a boarding school at Lansallos, only three miles to the west, that meant a separation from home that was not to his liking at such a tender age. The school under Thomas Sedgwick Cole was a success and moved to Winsor House, Pelynt, opening on 30 April 1798 with the intention of accommodating 70 pupils, though the venture was short-lived, closing at the end of the 1802 summer term (Carole Vivian, spring 1998, "Winsor Academy in Pelynt", *Cornwall Association of Local Historians Journal*, pp. 5-9). Here, however, Jonathan was able to take Latin lessons from Monsr. Arzell, "an emigrant Popish priest, one who had escaped from the horrors of the French revolution with the skin of his teeth". At this period he must have first become acquainted with Sir Harry Trelawny (by then a Catholic) who remained a personal friend and patient in adult life and who allowed Jonathan the use of his extensive library.

Trelawne, Pelynt, residence of Sir Harry Trelawny (1756-1834) and for some years the home of John Lewis Harding (1807-1893) who studied the rookery there in 1847-1848.

Photo by Lewis Harding c.1857

From Pelynt, Jonathan went to Bodmin Grammar School where, under Moses Morgan, "I had the opportunity of making some progress in the knowledge of the Classics". This was an important grounding, instilling in him a love of the Classics that culminated in his translation of Pliny's *Natural History*. "A week before Christmas 1849 I finished the translation and notes of the eighteenth Book of Pliny; exactly one half of the work". It was based on the only previous English edition, Philemon Holland's *Natural History of Gaius Plinius Secundus*, (1601, 2nd corrected edition in 1634). Part of Couch's translation was published by the Wernerian Club, London, in 1847, but the edition ended in mid-sentence in Book X, Chapter LIII on "The Propagation of Eggs: the Sitting of Birds, and their manner of Embrace". The two versions are not very different as the following extract from "Of the Cuckow" illustrates. Holland's translation:

In the spring, he commeth abroad, and by the beginning of the dog-daies, hides himselfe. These lay alwaies in other birds neasts, and most of all in the Stockdoves, commonly one egge and no more (which no other bird doth besides) and seldom twain.

Couch's translation:

In the Spring it cometh abroad, and at the rising of the Dog-star it hideth itself. It lays always in other Birds' Nests, and most of all in the Stock-doves', commonly one Egg only, which no other Bird doth besides; and seldom two.

How important the completed work might have been is hard to judge. J. Newsome (1964, *Pliny's Natural History, A Selection from Philemon Holland's Translation*, Oxford) is none too complimentary, describing it as "bowdlerized, emasculated, modernized, and generally given the mid-Victorian treatment, and it is as well the project lapsed". Newsome is naturally prejudiced and Couch's version would surely have been a more popular read for those not wishing to wallow in some of the Elizabethan phraseology. Couch did not lose his liking for the Classics and compiled

"Historical biographies of animals known to the Ancients". His MS is now in the Redpath Library at McGill Univeristy, Montreal, having been purchased from J. A. D. Bridger, the Penzance bookseller, before his 1924 sale. A microfilm copy exists in the Natural History Museum, London. The whole work comprises 606 pages (8 x 14 in) and one can only marvel at Couch's industry.

But to return to the young Jonathan. He left Bodmin in December 1803 and the following February resided with John Rice, "an eminent medical practitioner of East Looe, for the purpose of studying that profession". Rice was "deservedly esteemed as a very judicious man, of great practical knowledge in his profession". It was when he was at Looe in 1805 that Couch started his "Journal of Natural History" at the age of 16. The first year has only one entry, as do 1806 and 1809 (with none in the intervening years), and three in 1810. Not until 1815 does his small volume have more than a few pages, the result of his education and enforced absence from home. Rice died within a year or two and Couch completed his local education with a Mr Lawrence of Liskeard before entering, in 1808, the united schools of Guy's and St Thomas' hospitals in London. Jonathan had a high regard for the surgeon Mr Cooper, later Sir Astley Cooper (1768-1841), renowned for his expertise in the dissecting room where, until 1832, almost the only source of bodies came from the "body-snatchers".

After qualifying as a medical doctor, Jonathan returned to Polperro in 1810. He never seemed to yearn for pastures new. In the front of his *History of Polperro* is a Latin sentence, most probably composed by himself, that sums up his aspirations: *Nescio qua natale solum dulcedine cunctos ducit, et immemores non sinit esse sui* (I do not know by what charm all are drawn to our birthplace, and does not allow us to be unforgetful of it). Couch was immersed in his native village and the life and death of its people. "His care of the sick was exemplary and taken for granted by all (often without reward), as his efforts to improve the conditions of his people and to safeguard the fishermen's lives never ceased". It was said in Polperro that "if Dr Couch gave a patient up, it was no use to call anyone else in, you might just as well curl up your toes and die" according to Bertha Couch. "Q" recalled that patients to his house were at one time turned away from the front door "to a narrow backway because a garden spider had chosen to spin in the porch and the female must not be disturbed in her questionable career".

Couch married three times. First, on 14 October 1810, Jane Prynn Rundle of Porthallow, Lansallos, who tragically died at the premature birth of their only child Jane. After five years he married Jane Quiller of Polperro, by whom he had five sons and a daughter. Jane died on 6 September 1857, and on 23 October the following year he married at the age of sixty-nine, to the surprise of all, his third devoted wife, the good-looking twenty-two year old Sarah Lander Roose of Polperro who bore him three daughters, one of whom was his biographer Bertha.

With such family commitments, it is hardly surprising that Couch rarely wandered far from home. There is no evidence to show that he explored the whole of Cornwall, and it is clear from his writings that much of his information was obtained from others of a more peripatetic nature and odd notes collected from the local press or at meetings of the Penzance Natural History Society, The Royal Cornwall Polytechnic Society in Falmouth and the Royal Institution of Cornwall in Truro. In August 1839, for example, he visited "the west of the County, Falmouth, Penzance and Truro. His son, Richard Quiller Couch (1816-1863), resident in Penzance since 1843, lived in Chapel Street opposite the entrance to St Mary's churchyard. Jonathan stayed with him for a fortnight in September-October 1853. Notable people also visited Couch, including "Mr Alfred Tennyson, the poet". Jonathan visited him in Fowey on 19 June 1848, and the following day Peach took him to Polperro by boat. "He enquired

Jonathan Couch
From a pencil sketch dated 1824 by W. Dance in a private collection

about traditions, especially the great Arthur, his object in visiting the County being, to collect materials for a poem on that chief." The end result was, of course, *Idylls of the King* (1859) that did more than anything to establish Arthur's place in popular mythology. Couch, it should be remembered, was not only a naturalist but also a local historian and, to a small degree, an antiquarian.

"A vigorous constitution, careful habits, and healthful pursuits, carried him to the age of eighty-two", as Thomas Quiller Couch wrote in his sketch of Jonathan's life, though "insensibility to the advance of age" and annual attacks of bronchitis, the last "augmented by unavoidable exposure," brought about his peaceful end. On the morning of 13 April 1870, he sat in bed, "read his newspaper, despatched some correspondence on his favourite subjects; after which he fell into what seemed a quiet doze. He was left for a very short time. In this small space he *passed*; his end being apparently as tranquil as his course .... He was buried in the cemetery by the white-washed chapel at Mabel Burrow, Lansallos, "for once in its forlorn history crowded to the hedges. The crowd which followed him to the grave was, to a large extent, composed of fishermen, many of whose weather-bronzed faces were not unmarked by tears, and all indicating that a loss had befallen them" ("Q", 1944).

Jonathan Couch in top hat outside his house in Polperro

Photograph by Lewis Harding

c. *early 1860s*

THE COUCH MATERIAL AT THE ROYAL INSTITUTION OF CORNWALL

Jonathan Couch was the foremost 19th century naturalist of his native county. In the field of marine biology he was one of Britain's leading exponents. His greatest memorial is his four volume *History of British Fishes* (1862-65) illustrated with colour plates engraved from the author's own meticulous watercolours. Almost all of these paintings belong to the Royal Institution of Cornwall (RIC), having been purchased for £50 by J. D. Enys in 1906 and bequeathed to the RIC on his death in 1913. Couch's marine studies understandably eclipse his other works, but it should be remembered that his interests were extensive and that birds attracted his attention throughout his long and active life.

Couch had a long and close association with the RIC and it is fitting that the Institution now holds the most important collection of his published works and MSS. Much of this has only been acquired recently. On 13 December 1989, through the firm of Bernard Quaritch Ltd, the RIC purchased (with grant aid) firstly, at Sotheby's sale in New York, Couch's own copy of Parts I and II of his *A Cornish Fauna*, published by the RIC in 1838 and 1841, the whole bound in with various other papers relating to fish. Secondly, at the same sale, was purchased his MS "Cornish Birds" begun in 1829 and upon which the published account in Part I of *A Cornish Fauna* was based. These items had belonged to the Manhattan millionaire H. Bradley Martin, an Anglophile who died in 1988. Martin had been at Oxford in the 1920s and amassed a collection of over 10,000 volumes of rare works of English literature regarded as the finest in private hands in the world.

By coincidence in November 1990, with more generous grant aid, the RIC purchased volumes 1 to 10 of Couch's MS "Journal of Natural History" covering the period 1805-1862. These had been lost sight of, following their sale in 1924 by the Penzance bookseller J. A. D. Bridger, until they were discovered in the possession of Mr R. A. F. Palmer of Battle, Sussex, who had been given them as a boy by an aunt. Couch had compiled 12 volumes. The last two had been loaned by Couch's son Thomas Quiller Couch, after his father's death, to Francis Day the ichthyologist. Day published extracts from them in the now defunct journal *Land and Water*, but never returned them to Cornwall. After Day's death they were presented to Cheltenham Public Library on 31 December 1889 as part of the Day bequest by his two daughters as a memorial to their father. Through the kindness of the Gloucestershire County Librarian, volumes 11 and 12 were transferred to the RIC on 28 March 1992, thus uniting the full set for the first time in over a century.

On 19 May the same year, Couch's sketch book entitled "Figures of natural Objects", begun in 1836, was presented to the RIC by Mrs P. H. Edwards of Loughton, Essex, a great-great-granddaughter of Couch. The book contains a sketch of a Little Auk drawn on 18 January 1870, less than three months before his peaceful death on 13 April. The sketch shows the position of the bird's ear, a characteristic consequence of Couch's medical training that aroused his interest in the anatomy of animals in addition to the more prosaic observation of their occurrence. The same sketchbook includes several drawings of skulls and birds' heads in which the feathers have almost always been parted to reveal the position of the ear, as with the young Cuckoo drawn on 13 July 1854, the "ear opening upwards, the lower rim bony - rigid and standing out to catch the sound from above". Unfortunately, most of Couch's minor sketches, some in pencil, would not reproduce well and cannot be included in this book.

THE DEVELOPMENT OF ORNITHOLOGY AND COUCH'S SIGNIFICANCE

The study of ornithology in Britain slowly increased following the publication in 1544 of William Turner's *Avium Praecipuarum, quorum apud Plinium et Aristotelem mentio est, brevis & succincta historia*. Of importance here were not Turner's comments on the classical authorities, but his personal observations on the ninety-five species to which he gave English names. Cornishmen, too, played their part in the study of birds. Richard Carew's *Survey of Cornwall*, first published in 1602, contains the earliest account of the birds of any county, although his main consideration was whether most of them were edible or "content not the stomach". The Revd William Borlase, whose polymathic mind embraced the *Antiquities of Cornwall* (1754, 2nd ed. 1769) and *The Natural History of Cornwall* (1758), was more concerned with geology and mineralogy than with the feathered tribe, writing only one small section of six pages (Chapter XXI, *Of Birds*) - and figured only seven specimens.

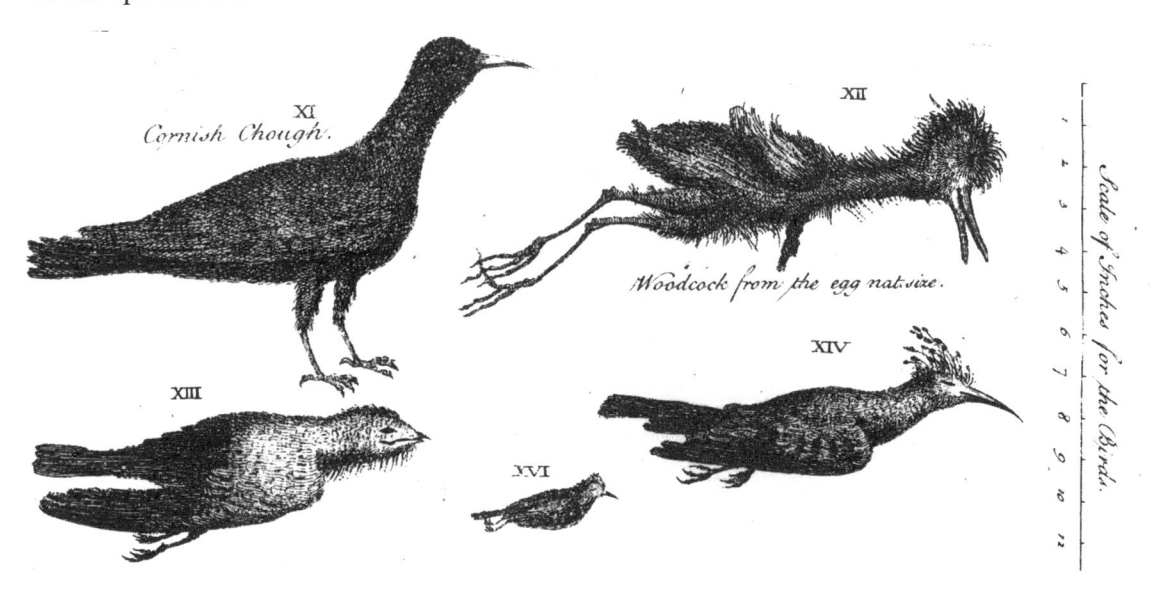

Birds from Borlase's Plate XXIV (see text for details)

Reproduced on the previous page are birds drawn from dead specimens, much inferior to his usual standard of illustrations: XI Cornish Chough; XII Woodcock from the egg; XIII Nightjar; XIV Hoopoe; XV Green Woodpecker (not shown) killed at Godolphin on 11 October 1757; XVI Goldcrest (see also **178** Storm-petrel).

Borlase, Plate XXIX, Storm-petrel

At the time of Jonathan Couch's birth, the number of useful books available on British birds was small - but times were changing. A Biological as well as an Industrial Revolution was taking shape. Interest in the natural world blossomed, perhaps one should say "blowed", to use the Revd Gilbert White's word, following his publication of *The Natural History of Selborne* in 1788. This work, which continues to appear in illustrated editions, inspired more people to take an interest in wildlife than any other single work in the English language. Couch was among those who took to heart White's dictum that "Every kingdom, every province, should have its own monographer" (Letter to Daines Barrington, 8 October 1770). Indeed, perhaps the greatest tribute to Couch is that given by G. T. Bettony in *The Dictionary of National*

Biography: "As a local naturalist whose conscientious and loving observation of nature has made a lasting impression on science, he deserves to rank beside Gilbert White". His knowledge on a wide range of subjects was enormous. "Q" recalled how "William Pengelly, FRS, famous for his exploration of Kent's Hole [Cavern] by Torquay with its relics of primitive man, once shook my childish hand with "My boy, I learned more of your grandfather than of any man or book."

Identification books of pocket size, illustrating in colour species of a particular geographical area, are a recent American invention. The pioneering *A Field Guide to the Birds* (of North America east of the Rockie Mountains), written and illustrated by Roger Tory Peterson, first appeared in 1934. Nothing comparable appeared in Britain until July 1952 when Collins published *The Pocket Guide to British Birds* written by R. S. R. Fitter and illustrated by R. A. Richardson. Now such guides are numerous, some much improved in quality. In the 18th and 19th centuries, lavishly illustrated works were produced. Mark Catesby's two folio volumes of the *Natural History of Carolina*, 1731-43, are the forerunner of many costly tomes beyond the purchasing power of all but the very wealthy. Among those of British interest are Eleazar Albin's three volume *Natural History of Birds*, 1738-60, and George Edwards' *Gleanings in Natural History*, in seven parts, 1743-60, the illustrations of which met with general approval amongst the few fortunate enough to have access to them. Couch could not have afforded these or the luxury of P. J. Selby's two folio volumes of *Illustrations of British Ornithology*, 1821-34, but he owned or had access to a number of standard works when he began his MS "Cornish Birds" in 1829. In common with general custom, he headed each species with bibliographical references. These show the books he consulted which themselves gave earlier scientific and vernacular names. Couch's "Cuckow", for example, is followed by "Cuculus Canorus, Turt. Lin. Vol 1 p250. Figure in Bewick's Br. Birds vol 1 p131. Fleming Br. An.

p90." In the last edition of Bewick (1826), the Cuckoo is on page 124 of vol. 1 (Land Birds) and headed by *Cuculus canorus*, Linn. [Linnaeus], and the French *Le Coucou* Buff. [G-L. L. Comte de Buffon, *Histoire Naturelle des Oiseaux*, 1770]. John Fleming's *A History of British Animals* was published in 1828. Some of the early references in Couch's "Journal of Natural History" are to quite obscure publications showing that he would read anything that might prove of interest. In June 1816, for example, he wrote that he had been informed of three species of titmice at Trelawne, but "I know only two Species, the greater, & a smaller not noticed in Gregory's Cyclopedia", George Gregory's *A Dictionary of Arts and Sciences*, 2 Vols., 1806-07 (2nd ed. 1813), Thomas Tagg, London.

Of the books most often referred to by Couch, by far the most influential in its day is Thomas Bewick's *A History of British Birds* (Vol. I, 1797, Vol. II, 1804).

Thomas Bewick (1753-1828)

Bewick supervised six editions, a clear indication of its popularity. Couch sometimes referred specifically to the last edition of 1826, as under Glaucus Gull in his 1838 *A Cornish Fauna*. Bewick was a wood engraver, technically one of the best, who spent seven years of "severe confinement and application" preparing the illustrations. It is not always realised that most of the text was not by Bewick. The text for Vol. I (Land Birds) was by Ralph Beilby, his partner and former master in their Newcastle printing works. After Beilby's retirement, Henry Cotes, Vicar of Bedlington, assisted with the text for Vol. II (Water Birds). In spite of their popularity, Bewick's volumes had their limitations: all the illustrations are monochrome, differences of sex and age are ignored or sometimes assigned to different species because of the general lack of knowledge then prevalent. However charming the engravings, not all are infallible guides to identification: compare, for example, the warblers figured above **88** Chiffchaff and the gulls under **188** Herring Gull. Errors were bound to occur, as Couch points out in his account of the Little Gull: "Bewick was under a mistake in reference to this Species, when he figur'd the Young of the Kittiwake in its place; as he seems indeed, to admit in a letter to me." Ironically, Couch's own drawing of a Little Gull in his "Cornish Birds" turns out to be a Sabine's Gull, emphasising the problems of identification encountered by naturalists in the early 19th century. Bewick's small vignettes of country scenes have stood the test of time far better than his birds.

In spite of their shortcomings, Bewick's volumes instilled a greater interest in birds, certainly until the mid-1840s, than any other work except White's *Selborne*. His vignettes of rural life may have been the inspiration for Couch's less competent pen sketches scattered through his manuscript "Cornish Birds". It may be no coincidence that Couch's rather curious owl with flattened ear-tufts resembles in its pose Bewick's superior rendering of a Long-eared Owl, or that Bewick had presented

Couch with a copy of his *Fables of Æsop* (1818) with its equally appealing illustrations. The two had a great respect for each other. A letter to Couch from Bewick on 2 April 1822 survives in the Laing Gallery in Newcastle, though this deals with fish. Bewick contemplated publishing a book on the History of British Fishes, though he was prevented from doing so by personal circumstances. Of Couch he wrote: "Your labours will, I hope be a great acquisition ... & I impatiently wait for the arrival of your manuscript & Drawings; these I shall acknowledge in any way that may be most satisfactory and agreable to yourself, as to my other works you shall have them sent in any way you may please to direct."

Couch knew that Bewick had received specimens of the Cravat (Canada Goose) and Spur-winged Goose from Henry Mewburn (1780-1834), land agent of the Port Eliot Estate in St Germans from 1812 to the autumn of 1829. Details of these birds, and others from Cornwall, are contained in a letter from Mewburn to George Townshend Fox who published them in *The Synopsis of the Newcastle Museum* (1827). Couch is not known to have met Mewburn, though his friend Clement Jackson must have done so (see Spur-winged Goose, **220**).

For birds that were not known to Bewick or had been confused by him, Couch referred to Eyton in his *A Cornish Fauna* (1838): Bluethroat, Carolina Cuckow, Alpine swift, Stock Dove, Black Stork, Temminck's Stint, Surf Scoter, Little Gull, Arctic Jaeger, and Cinereous Shearwater. T. C. Eyton's *History of the Rarer British Birds* (1836) was published as a supplement to Bewick's volumes and provided, "at a moderate cost", woodcuts by Mr Mark of Wellington as an aid to identification. Also used by Couch was Leonard Jenyns' *Manual of British Vertebrate Animals* (1835), references to which gradually replace those of Fleming's *A History of British Animals* (1828). Jenyns gave more information on species' status than did Fleming, albeit in only two or three lines. Couch recognised Jenyns' superiority as he kept abreast of current literature, a trait also made clear by his references to Yarrell.

William Yarrell (1784-1856)

William Yarrell corresponded with Couch, both having an abiding interest in fish and birds. Couch rarely wandered far from Polperro, and it says much of his respect for Yarrell that he visited him and stayed with him at his London home from 19 to 28 August 1835 and again for a fortnight in May 1849. Yarrell's *History of British Fishes* was completed in 1836 leaving him free to work on *A History of British Birds*. This was published in 37 parts at intervals of two months, the first issued in July 1837 and the last in May 1843. The second edition in three volumes also appeared in 1843. Couch began his MS "Cornish Birds" long before Yarrell's work appeared, but in his 1838, *A Cornish Fauna*, the first six members of "The Falcon Tribe" (Golden Eagle to Merlin) which open the account, are given page numbers up to 48 in Yarrell's Volume I, the only ones available to Couch as he wrote his text in the summer or autumn of 1837. Couch's 1841 "Appendix" to *A Cornish Fauna* (a modified version of a paper to the British Association of the Advancement of Science held in Plymouth in that year), and his "Supplement" of 1844, include references to all three of Yarrell's volumes. Yarrell's work remained a standard reference well into the 20th century in the enlarged edition in four volumes issued between 1871 and 1874.

COUCH'S LOCAL CONTACTS

The names scattered through Couch's MS "Journal of Natural History" show that neighbours, from the well-to-do to the poorest fisherfolk of Polperro, were ready and willing to take him interesting specimens for identification, to describe to him unusual birds they had seen, or nests they had encountered. Dr Jonathan Couch was on good terms with his patients, many of whom he would have helped to bring into the world. Two Polperro men named are William and John Minards to whom he was related on his mother's side: "John is too accurate an Observer to be mistaken" in his identification of an Alpine Swift, wrote Couch. William's name appears frequently when observations were made on the nesting sites and behaviour of such common birds as the Stonechat, Wren and Dipper, nor can there be any doubt that he saw the first authentic Bluethroat in Cornwall in 1836. To some extent, Couch was like a spider waiting for titbits to fly to him, no doubt because William, a shoe maker, and local fishermen found a little more time for outdoor observations than the busy doctor.

John Minards

William Minards

An amateur scientific friend was Charles William Peach (1800-1886), a "riding officer" of the Coast Guard service who lived at Gorran from 1835 to 1845 and then at Fowey as Customs Officer. He was popularly known as "the Cornish geologist" in spite of having been born in Northamptonshire. His interest in birds was relatively slight. In 1837 he discovered a Nightingale at Caerhays (see **252**), and rowed Couch up the Fowey River in May 1848 to look at the heronries. Their friendship grew out of a common interest in fossils and marine fauna, but close contact ceased when Peach was removed from Fowey to Peterhead, Scotland, at Christmas time the following year.

Couch's closest ornithological companion was his "excellent friend Clement Jackson" of East Looe, a batchelor, chemist, amateur taxidermist, "the last of the friends or Quakers in that Town" who died aged about 53 in 1856. The wanton killing of wild birds is now rightly condemned, but it was a virtual necessity in the early 19th century when the general rule was "What's hit is history, what's missed is mystery", as the famous Harry Forbes Witherby had engraved on his book-plate. Advances in ornithology necessitated the close examination of specimens in the hand, as Couch did, often in company with Clement Jackson. It was through such work that the number of birds on the British and Irish list increased from about 240 in 1800 to 380 a century later, and the difficulties of distinguishing different species in varying states of plumage were gradually overcome.

Little is known of the retiring Clement Jackson who "never paraded his knowledge", as recalled by a Mrs A. C. P. (*Hardwick's Science-Gossip*, 1 August 1867, pp. 182-3). Before 1840 he became "acquainted with the principle of the aquarium: how a judicous admixture of plants and animals will keep each other in health ... His little shop was an *omnium gatherum* and not the least interesting portion of its furniture were the odd-looking tubs, jars, and bottles in which were placed the plants and animals whose natural habits he desired, as far as posssible, to observe."

Jackson made periodic excursions to west Cornwall — Swanpool, Falmouth, being a favourite haunt where he shot a number of birds that he mounted with great skill. Some he presented to the Royal Institution of Cornwall, though none survives there now. In May 1856, Jackson was on his way west and had got as far as St Austell when he was taken ill on the 25th, dying two days later of "an Aneurism of the descending Aorta". His death greatly saddened Couch, closing his "intimate connection with Looe, as no one there besides cares much for natural Science — some exception may be made in favour of Mr Stephen Clogg — but no one else" (MS, Memorials of the family of Couch", pp. 102-3). Clogg followed the same profession as Couch, but did not pursue natural history with the same dedication, although he took a greater interest in insects than his more famous neighbour. Clogg was born in 1812 in Liskeard and practised as a doctor there until moving in 1840 to Looe where he remained until his death on 19 November 1890. Yarrell's death on 1 September 1856, so soon after the demise of Jackson, led Couch to write:

> Unhappy he who latest feels the blow,
>
> Whose eyes have wept o'er every friend laid low,
>
> Dragged lingering on from partial death to death,
>
> Till dying, all he can resign is breath.

On 5 October 1829, Clement Jackson, Jonathan Couch and the Revd J. Lakes submitted a short paper on "Rare or uncommon Birds observed in Cornwall" (*Loudon's Magazine of Natural History*, Vol. 3, pp. 175-177). John Lakes, born in St Austell on 10 September 1801, had an early interest in birds when Curate of Liskeard (1827-39). He was noted for "his many good sketches of interesting objects in the neighbourhood" (J. Allen, 1856, *History of the Borough of Liskeard*, p. 184), but apart from the above contribution and an earlier note on "A dark looking Water Bird" (see Surf Scoter, **206**), published nothing else of ornithological interest in his long and active life; he died on 26 March 1891.

Couch made extensive notes on the plumage and anatomy of specimens, comparing them critically with the illustrations in Bewick's *British Birds*. Charles Dixon, a prolific author of popular appeal, in his first published work, *Rural Bird Life* (1880), was one of the first to advocate the use of a first-class telescope (an instrument Couch employed by 1816 if not before) or the then relatively new field-glasses that Couch probably never possessed. Yet even Dixon described in detail how to blow eggs and what size of shot should be used to kill various species, the whole tempered only with the hope that his instruction should not "cause a wanton expense of life ... Oh, then! deep indeed will be the regret that I ever wrote them". A far cry this, nevertheless, from the famous American artist-naturalist John James Audubon (1785-1851) who is credited with the remark, "I call birds few when I shoot less than a hundred a day". Couch rarely killed any birds himself (see Bullfinch, **51**) and he was at pains to care for and observe the habits of captured birds that came his way, such as the Wigeon caught by boys in January 1836. Thomas Quiller Couch, in a footnote to his late father's *The History of Polperro* (1871, p. 29), makes the following pertinent and amusing remark of his visit there in 1870: "I was gratified to see so soon after the passing of the Act for the Preservation of Sea Birds [1869; see further under Kittiwake, **192**], the great increase in the number of Gulls, and their growing trustfulness of man. Crowding in the harbour, or wading at the edge of the beach surrounded by men and boys, they were busily employed in picking up the garbage which gave Polperro the reproachful name of Polstink".

COUCH'S CATALOGUE OF CORNISH BIRDS

The order in which Couch deals with species in his MS "Cornish Birds" and in *A Cornish Fauna* is quite different from current usage and closely follows that adopted by W. Turton, 1807, *British Fauna*. Classification now aims to show the evolutionary relationship between species, families and other taxa, and progresses from the more primitive to the more advanced. So far as British birds are concerned, the sequence now begins with the divers and ends with the buntings. Such a system had no place in the early 19th century when all species were believed to be immutable products of a single glorious act of creation. Suffice it to say that Couch and his antecedents followed similar systems that differed little from the one devised by the great John Ray (1627-1705) in *The Ornithology of Francis Willughby*, published in Latin in 1676 and in 1678 in English "enlarged with many Additions throughout".

Ray's method was logical, sensible, and was adopted with little change by Carl von Linné (Linnaeus, 1707-78) who did more than anyone to sort out the contemporary muddle of classification. Ray was concerned with the external similarities and differences between species. He divided birds into the *Terrestrial* and *Aquatic*, subdividing the birds in these groups according to the form of their beaks and feet. Couch, like Ray, begins with the same species – diurnal birds of prey followed by owls – but unlike a good orchestra they end on different notes. We can ignore such taxonomic discord. In the following "Catalogue of Cornish Birds", Couch's preliminary page references to the works of Turton, Bewick and other authorities are ignored, as are the now defunct scientific names he employed, except in those cases where it has been necessary to note them. The vernacular name used by Couch is followed by the now standardised English name and the current scientific name adopted by the British Ornithologists' Union in 1992. Couch's peculiarities of spelling and punctuation have been largely retained, although it is not always clear when he intended a full stop rather than a comma. Where commas have been left out (as in Jacksons for Jackson's), or where there should be one to indicate a missing letter (kill'd, for killed), a comma has been inserted for clarity.

Extracts from Couch's "Journal of Natural History" follow in square brackets in smaller type, as do my own comments and references to newspapers and other publications. In most cases, these form the largest section for each species.

Roger D. Penhallurick
Truro

Jonathan Couch
holding the tusk of an African Babiroussa (wild boar)
Collodion photograph taken at Trelawne, Pelynt by
Lewis Harding in October 1856

ABBREVIATIONS

J	Couch's unpublished "Journal of Natural History" (1805-1870). Roman numerals indicate the volume number and arabic numerals the page. Extracts within [ ] brackets only consist of the volume and page.
JRIC	*Journal of the Royal Institution of Cornwall.* The Institution runs the Royal Cornwall Museum, formerly the County Museum and Art gallery.
MM	*The Monthly Magazine.*
MNH	*Loudon's Magazine of Natural History.*
Pz	*Report of the Penzance Natural History & Antiquarian Society.*
PZS	*Proceedings of the Zoological Society of London.*
RCG	*The Royal Cornwall Gazette* newspaper. Dates show the month in roman numerals.
RCPS	*Report of the Royal Cornwall Polytechnic Society*, Falmouth.
RRIC	*Report of the Royal Institution of Cornwall* (predates publication of the annual *Journal*).
TN	*The Naturalist; a popular monthly magazine.*
TPI	*Transactions of the Plymouth Institution.*
WB	*West Briton* newspaper. Dates show the month in roman numerals.
Z	*Zoologist*

CATALOGUE OF CORNISH BIRDS

BIRDS OF PREY

FALCONS

1 Ringtail'd Eagle [Golden Eagle *Aquila chrysaetos*]

A specimen of what I believe to be this Species was shot in the Parish of Lanteglos by Fowey.

[This was an immature Golden Eagle shot "a few days ago" in November 1810 by Mr Rain of Tredake, "whilst feeding on the carcase of a sheep" (*WB*, 23 xi). The full description, also published in Dougdale, 1819, *The New British Traveller*, was compared with specimens in Bolton Museum in 1973 confirming the identification of the only authenticated Golden Eagle from Cornwall. "Ring-tailed" implies an immature bird, originally believed to be a distinct species. Couch wrote of "One, clearly made out, was near Trelawny [Trelawne, Pelynt] in the end of December (1858); & was shot at. It was afterwards seen in St Martin's Parish" (x, 418). This record and reports of a Golden Eagle at Trelowarren, Merthen, and St Buryan from December to February 1858-59 were not confirmed. All such records for Cornwall are suspect and most probably refer to Buzzards, such as the supposed eagle's nest on the cliff at St Buryan in 1831 (*WB*, 24 vi), or "the eagle" startled from its nest at High Cove, near Mawagn Porth on 4 July 1833 (R. L. Brett, 1979, *Barclay Fox's Journal*, p.50).]

2 Kite [Red Kite *Milvus milvus*]

Very rare; but I have heard of a few specimens.

[Couch may be referring to those recorded by Mr James of St Keverne (*MM*, xii 1808) who "never saw but three, and those in severe winters". The Trelowarren gamebook records a pair shot on the estate in November 1809. Two more presented to Truro Museum in 1835-36 had been shot near Mevagissey. In his *Journal* (i, 121) for 1816, Couch includes the Kite in a list of birds "I have discovered of my knowledge to be found in Cornwall" and "Such as reside thro' the Year", though there is no proof that the species was resident in the County. Early records must be treated with caution because, as Edward Moore noted in 1830 (*TPI*, p. 296), in south Devon, Common Buzzards were "erroneously termed Kites by the common people". Couch includes few other references to Kites:

One "flew over my garden July 19 1832" (vi, 26).

"Mr Tucker informs me that he shot a Kite Sepr 1 1848 - It was a Bird of large size, & his attention was particularly directed to its forked tail. It was in the Parish of St Germans" (ix, 189). Tucker was the carrier who regularly travelled between Polperro and Plymouth.]

3 Peregrine Falcon [*Falco peregrinus*]

I insert this Species on the authority of the Revd. J. Lakes in the Nat. Mag. of Mr Loudon, Vol 3, p175 [1830]. [Added later] I have seen a Specimen & heard of more.

[His comment proves the scarcity of this species in south-east Cornwall then as now, though J. C. Bellamy (1839, p. 199) noted its occasional occurrence at Whitsand Bay, south-east Cornwall. Couch recorded one shot on 12 July 1832, but gave no locality (vi, 26), while on 2 May 1856 he noted that one had been shot at Trelawne, Pelynt, "where it had knocked down a Rook (x, 300). Peregrines always favoured the higher cliffs of the north and west, but the Revd Lakes believed that the species, locally called "the Wicked Hawk", had nested "annually a few years since" in cliffs near Charlestown, his identification based on the remains of a stuffed specimen that he found nailed to a barn door.]

4 Buzzard [Common Buzzard *Buteo lagopus*]

I observe of a young Buzzard that when it seizes hold it is not by bending or closing its toes, but by incurving its Claws only, which being sharp, crooked & moving with strong muscles are turn'd on and darted into the object, while the toes remaining straight offer a strong opposing force. So powerful is this grasp that I could scarcely extricate my hand from its grasp. It is probable that all Birds of prey act in the same manner. Very common.

Ruysch says it feeds on some herbs, as selerea [Celery], asperula [probably Sweet Woodruffe] & matrisylva [Woodruffe sp.?]; mice, frogs, lizards, serpents, slugs, caterpillars.

There seems to be enmity between this Bird & the Crow.

[Comments on seizing prey were made in July 1829 by a bird in Couch's possession (v, 75). There is no evidence that herbs form part of the Buzzard's diet which largely comprises small mammals and variable amounts of other creatures. Frederick Ruysch, a 17th century anatomist at Leiden, was author of *Thesaurus Animalium Primus*, a rare work published in Dutch and Latin in 1710.]

5 Moor Buzzard [Eurasian Marsh Harrier *Circus aeruginosus*]

Rare; a Specimen kill'd near St Austle, January 1832.

[It is possible that Moor Buzzard was applied to other harriers. January is an unusual date, though not unknown, for a Marsh Harrier to be seen, but most appropriate for the Hen Harrier (see under "Ash coloured Harrier" below). Couch saw a Marsh Harrier, newly set up by Clement Jackson, that had been killed on the moor near Liskeard a day or two before 28 December 1853 (x, 180). The St Austell bird is mistakenly noted "as common near St Austell" (vi, 20).]

6 Sparrow Hawk [Eurasian Sparrowhawk *Accipiter nisus*]
Common in woods.

[This raptor was probably rather scarce around Polperro, Couch recording it only twice in his *Journal*. In the spring of 1847, one "broke its neck by a headlong rush against a wall". It gave him the opportunity to describe the "firm overhanging bone plate" that protected the eye, and "a projecting caruncle" (fleshy excrescence) on its longest toe, "more projecting ... than in the Kestrel ... evidently calculated for great sensibility of touch, but preventing pleasurable or easy walk on a hard substance" (ix, 110). In 1834 he had been assured that one had "repeatedly been seen to dip into our River after Trout" (vi, 123). This is so extraordinary a record that it may be a case of mistaken identity; most prey are small birds with a few per cent of mammals. Kestrels, however, have caught "small fish from the surface of water like a tern" (L. Brown, 1976, *British Birds of Prey*, p. 203).]

7 Fishing Eagle [Osprey *Pandion haliaetus*]

[No information given, and only "Scarce" in his published 1838 account. Ospreys have long been familiar as passage migrants, mainly in August and September. Clement Jackson told Couch in 1831, on the authority of the Inspector of Lights, "that a pair of Fishing Eagles, as figur'd by Bewick, built a nest near the Lizard Point either last year, & or the {year} past before: both Birds were taken in Gins" (v, 154). Yarrell (1843, Vol. I, p. 24) published the account as "Mr Couch sends me word that the species is believed to breed every year on the rocks about the Lizard". Because the birds were captured, the record is probably correct, though Jackson does not appear to have seen the birds himself. In northern Europe, Ospreys normally nest in trees, using cliffs and rocky islets from the Mediterranean southwards. Walter Moyle recorded that he shot one in 1717 which had two young and an egg in a nest on the Long Stone between Portwrinkle and Downderry. Courtney (1845, p. 25) refers to one in E.H. Rodd's collection from the Lizard area, presumably the bird killed at Helford in the spring of 1838 (*RRIC*, 1838, p. 40) and almost certainly the one illustrated by J.T. Blight (1861, p. 92).

Couch wrote that a specimen "was caught alive at Moors Water near Liskeard" on 14 October 1848 (ix, 154), "as I learn from the Cornwall Gazette" (*RCG*, 20 x). Nicholas Hare, writing on

Osprey, after Blight

6 October, said it was captured with little injury using a gin on top of a pole 12 to 14 feet long "this morning at Moorswater Lodge ... it had been seen on several previous days about the grounds; the trout in the fishing pond no doubt allured it". Perched on railings in front of the house, "it had a noble appearance and looked resigned, though sad" (*Pz*, 1848, p. 212). Clement Jackson told Couch that a bird of the year was shot at, but flew off, about the Millpool at Looe in the last week of June 1855 (x, 256).]

8 Henharrier [Hen Harrier *Circus cyaneus*]

[No information given, nor in his published 1838 account. This suggests that Couch was not familiar with the Hen Harrier. See under Moor Buzzard above and the following entry.]

9 Ash coloured Falcon [Montagu's Harrier *Circus pygargus*]

I saw a specimen, January 1832.

[This harrier is a summer visitor first distinguished from the other harriers by Col. George Montagu in 1802. Couch's specimen is more likely to have been a wintering Hen Harrier (see under "Moor Buzzard" above).]

10 Kestrel [Common Kestrel *Falco tinnunculus*]

Common in cliffs. Creshawk in Cornwall. [Added later] It feeds much on beetles: throwing up the Elytera in pellets from the stomach.

[It was Clement Jackson's tame bird in 1837 that threw up pellets from "soft animal food" (vii, 263). Dor beetles (Geotrupidae) are the only beetles taken in Britain and may constitute over 40 per cent of a Kestrel's diet from autumn to spring. Larger prey is fed to the chicks by the female, tearing it into smaller pieces to feed to the nestlings bill-to-bill, as William Minards discovered when watching local cliff-nesting birds in 1835 (vii, 35). This method of feeding is common to all newly-hatched raptors (L. Brown, 1976, *British Birds of Prey*, p. 331). About 20 per cent of prey consists of small birds. In the spring of 1845, John Pucky observed Wheatears flying across the Channel and saw "our common brown Hawk - which must be the Kestrel - fly off the land, about a mile, & when a Wheatear came in sight from seawards, it chas'd it to the land; after many efforts the Wheatear escap'd; when the hawk again flew off, waited until another appeared which it succeeded in capturing" (ix, 30).

In 1840, Couch records (viii, 142) "14 Oct. Captn. Walcott informs me that when at Veryan on Sunday the 11th. the Revd Mr Trist took him to see a Nest of this bird in a cliff near Portlooe {Portloe} having two eggs". Couch's earliest account of the habits of a bird of prey concerns the Kestrel: 3 February 1816. "When this Bird looks for prey, keeping itself steady in the air, it is usually over the beginning of the descent of a hill, & not over the valley, by which means it sees all before it, in all the valley. When nothing is to be seen, it flies across the valley to the beginning of the descent of the next hill, & there again looks out" (i, 98).

Creshawk was a name confined to Cornwall, perhaps a variant of dialect Cristel-hawk derived from Old French *cristel*, now *crécerelle*.]

11 Merlin [*Falco columbarius*]

Scarce, & in winter only. [Added later] Marlion, of Carew.

[Richard Carew (1602) lists it as one of the birds of prey (Old English, as also Marlin). E. H. Rodd called it "not uncommon ... frequents the outskirts of moors, bordering cultivated land" and knew of examples from Madron and Gulval near Penzance before 1850 (*Pz*, 1850, p. 401). Couch does not mention this species in his *Journal*.]

The word Hawk is deriv'd from the Anglosaxon name of the Bird, Hafoc, & is explained by our corresponding word havock.

[The old Norse is *haukr* and Old English *hafoc* like the Dutch *havik*.]

OWLS

12 Longear'd Owl [Long-eared Owl *Asio otus*]

Scarce. [Added later] One came down the Chimney at Trelawny [Trelawne, Pelynt].
[The addition was incorrectly placed under Short-eared Owl. The account in his *Journal* (viii, 52) entered sometime before 16 September 1839, clearly states that a "Longear'd Owl came through the Chimney of the Hall at Trelawny house in the evening, about ten days since. It remained for the night, & was set at liberty on the following morning". A "Curious Bird" shot "last week" by Mr. Frost, gamekeeper to Lord Grenville, at Boconnoc was clearly a Long-eared Owl, its "two strong feathers projecting about three inches over each eye" (*WB*, 24 i 1827). This species remains a rare passage migrant and winter visitor to Cornwall with breeding records in 1924, 1927, 1934 and 1985.]

13 [Northern Hawk Owl *Surnia ulula*]

Inserted later under its old scientific name

Strix funerea; caught a few miles from the Coast of Cornwall by a coasting vessel; it came into the hands of Mr Thompson of Belfast.
[This was a bird of the American race *S. ulula caparoch*, the first British record, captured alive but exhausted in the rigging of a collier bound for Waterford in March 1830. It was kept alive at Waterford for several weeks and after its death passed to a Dr Burkitt who presented it to Trinity College, Dublin. William Thompson of Belfast published an account of it in *PZS*, 1835, p. 77.]

14 Short Ear'd owl [Short-eared Owl *Asio flammeus*]

Scarce & in winter only.
[One "very thin" was found dead in a field on 3 December 1840 (viii, 152). Its status remains unchanged. Couch described the large structure of the ear of this species on 23 January 1867 (xii, 26), but it is not stated if this was from a local specimen. A later insert which refers to the Long-eared Owl is given above.]

15 White Owl [Barn Owl *Tyto alba*]

Common. On reference to a specimen it is evident that Bewick has err'd in making the wings extend so far beyond the tail; since they terminate together.
[At rest the wings do extend beyond the tail, though less than Bewick's engraving suggests.]

Barn Owl, after Bewick

16 Tawny Owl [*Strix aluco*]

[No entry, but see next species.]

17 Aluco Owl [Tawny Owl *Strix aluco*]

This species has been judg'd to be only a variety of the Tawny Owl, & therefore is not notic'd by Bewick or Fleming. Its distinguishing marks are black iris, first quill feathers serrate. The dark colour of the irides enables it to bear the light well; & hence I have known it to have been kill'd on the wing at midday.

[The iris is a dark brown. Couch ignores the supposed Aluco Owl in his 1838 account. Confusion had arisen because Thomas Pennant had seen a specimen with yellow irides, an error made by the taxidermist. Couch kept a Tawny Owl in captivity in December 1820 (iii, 91).]

The common name of these Birds is derived either from the Latin Ululo, or the Corresponding English term, to howl.

[Owl is dervied from Latin *ulula* via Old Teutonic *uwala* and Old English *ule*. Howl appears in Middle English as *hulen* or *houlen*, perhaps from the cry of the bird.]

Shrikes

18 Great Ashcolour'd Shrike [Great Grey Shrike *Lanius excubitor*]

I have seen the fragments of a Specimen shot at Colon [Colan] near St Columb; & have been inform'd of an instance of its breeding in Cornwall.

[The remains were seen at Clement Jackson's on 2 October 1829, a few months after it had been shot (v, 91). The record published in 1830 (*MNH*, p. 175) puts the year as 1828.

Couch recorded in April 1847 "that Mr Abraham, a dealer in Birds at Liskeard informs me, that in March last, the greater Shrike was shot near that Town, he possess'd the Bird, & believes it to be that Species" (ix, 111). The Great Grey Shrike has never been proved to breed in Britain.]

19 Red back'd Shrike [Red-backed Shrike *Lanius collurio*]

Appears near Looe about the 5th of May; & is not uncommon thro' the summer [*MNH*, 1830, p. 175].

[The species regularly nested in small numbers in east Cornwall in the 19th century but is now only a rare passage migrant. On 25 August 1845 (ix, 45), Couch described in detail a young bird taken "on one of our Drift Boats in the night after midnight, about 5 miles from land - I conclude it to be migrating". Nicholas Hare of Liskeard wrote in September 1849 that about two months previously a party of bird-catchers "went into a field near our church, with linnets and limed twigs, to catch some young finches that frequented there. Whilst the birds were 'calling,' a female red-backed shrike dashed down amongst them, and was caught on one of the twigs" (*Pz*, 1849, p. 315).]

Birds of the Pie Kind

20 Raven [Common Raven *Corvus corax*]

Builds in Cliffs near the Sea, & is a great Devourer of young Rabits, Turkeys, & Chicken.

[Ravens are omnivourous with carrion meat, rather than live prey, being the most important part of their diet. In the spring of 1839, Couch watched the reaction of the parents when young birds were taken captive from the nest: "They seek about with great eagerness & silent assiduity, & when they have found them they become exceedingly clamorous, flying down close to them, & seemingly inviting them to come away; but not - or very rarely - alighting on the ground near them, & in no one instance bringing them food in their captivity. They are thus eager for the space of a day; but no longer, & finding the Young not able to go with them to solitude, they visit them no more" (viii, 41).]

21 Carrion Crow [*Corvus corone*]

With us sometimes call'd the Town Crow. It lives in pairs thro' the Year, & commonly returns to its usual haunts to sleep.

["Our Postman, who is a trustworthy Authority," told Couch in 1867 that when driving along the road he had seen a rabbit being killed by a stoat. "But while he stopped to witness the progress of this affair a Crow that seems to have been looking out for something to satisfy its hunger, became also an interested Spectator of what was going on. Unterrified therefore by the hazardous Nature of the Act, its resolution was immediately taken, and down it pounced upon the Rabbit, with an effort to snatch it from the formidable jaws of the Stoat. If left to themselves it is uncertain in what manner this Contest would have ended; for if it had turned on the intruder the teeth of the Stoat would have proved themselves formidable weapons. But the third party by this time thought himself also an interested party; - he advanced therefore and snatched the already dead Rabbit from both of them" (xii, 52-53).

Carrion Crows have a very varied diet. Edward Minards told Couch in 1835 that he had seen one "carry off in its Bill, all the eggs, one by one, of a Shag from the nest" (vi, 158). In 1850 he learned of two more examples of the bird's catholic tastes: "An intelligent labourer assures me that Crows are at this time {about June} employed in digging up the new potatoes; just as Rooks do. And William Minards informs me that he saw a Crow catch a Trout in the Looe Canal. The water at that place was deeper than the Crow was high, & the bank sloping. The Bird was walking along & made a dart at it; throwing the fish up the bank to the distance of 8 or 10 feet; where it devour'd it at its leisure" (ix, 200). Crows have been known to completely immerse themselves in deep water.]

22 Hooded Crow [subspecies *Corvus corone cornix*]

Scarce, & in winter only: visiting us in those Seasons when the Shortear'd Owl appears. Seen on the wing the Hooded Crow seems to have its feathers hanging more loosely about it.

[This subspecies is seen more rarely now in Cornwall than in the early 19th century. Early in 1840, Couch noted that "Royston Crows have been more abundant than usual this winter; several having been seen or kill'd" (viii, 77). His only other record is of "an old bird, deep in moult", shot near Looe on 17 August 1850 (ix, 207).

Royston Crow was the name applied to it by Eleazar Albin (*Natural History of Birds*, 1731-38) due to numbers having been seen about Royston and Newmarket in winter. Market Jew Crow was the usual Cornish dialect, named after Marazion (*Marghasyou* = Thursday Market) where birds were "Formerly abundant on Marazion Green" according to E. H. Rodd (*Pz*, 1850, p. 413). Borlase (1758. p. 245) found them there "fond of the products of the beach" from October to March.]

23 Rook [*Corvus frugilegus*]

There is a fine Rookery at Trelawny & a smaller ones at Duloe, [and] Fowey.

[The rookery at Trelawne was the largest ever recorded in Cornwall. Couch instructed Lewis Harding, as a mental therapy, to make daily records of the habits of the birds for a year from 28 August 1847 to 30 August following. This is the earliest known study in such detail of any single species of bird, perhaps anywhere. The first nest was finished on 30 February and all were completed on 15 April when the total number was 478 nests. The MS is entitled "Life in a Rookery collected for Jonathan

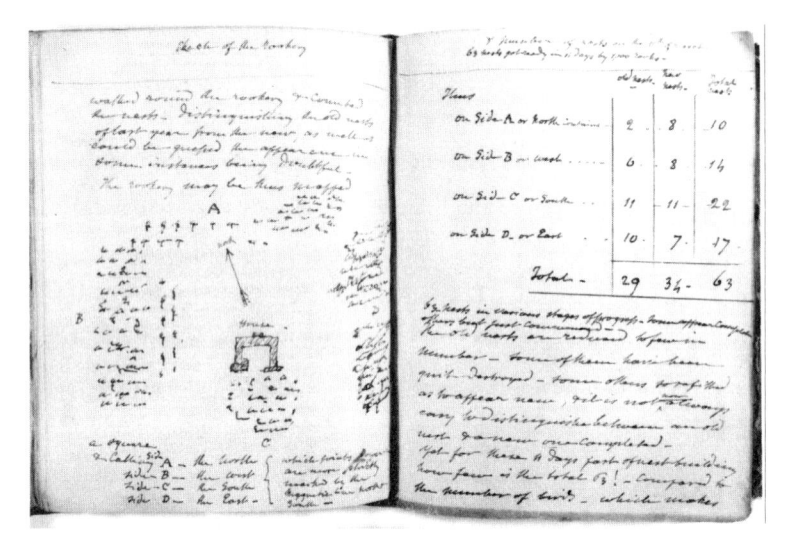

Pages from J. Lewis Harding's 'Life of a Rookery'

showing the site of the Rookery at Trelawne, Pelynt, and the number of nests built on 11 March 1847

Couch" and must have been suggested by Couch when his *Illustrations of Instinct* was published at the end of August 1847, a work that had occupied him "nearly two years in writing". He refers to the Rook five times. He was particularly interested in their habit of nesting close to man, as "in the neighbourhood of some dignified mansion" (p. 333, also pp. 105, 213-214); the close association of Jackdaws and Rooks (p. 166); the ability of Rooks to discover cockchafer grubs "at some depth below the soil" (p. 194); and the theft of building materials from neighbours' nests (pp. 333-334). Harding also told Couch in 1850 about the habit of the male Rook in bowing to the female "before they fly off together" to collect nest lining (ix, 191).

Alfred Newton in the 4th edition of Yarrell's *British Birds* (1876-82) wrote that "A good monograph of the Rook could not fail to be as interesting as its compilation would be laborious". Yarrell did not say this in the earlier editions of his work, so neither he nor Newton can have been aware of Harding's monumental study. It is unfortunate that Couch had not brought it to Yarrell's attention. It was not until 1870 that T. Q. Couch wrote in the volume on 1 May, soon after his father's death, that the author was Lewis Harding. Although Harding had taken up photography by October 1856, he did not take pictures of the rookery, though he did make a rough sketch plan of the site in his survey. It was probably soon after 1856 that Harding moved his studio to Polperro.

Stephen Clogg told Couch in 1867 that the rookery at Duloe, "of moderate size", had been known to him for fifty years. "Last year it appeared to have become less numerous: & this year it seems to be forsaken" (xii, p. 36). Few rookeries in Cornwall now exceed 100 nests, most containing a few dozen. The largest in the 1975-76 survey was at Tresillian Barton, Newlyn East, with 249 nests, but for official purposes this counted as three rookeries because the groups were more than 100 metres apart.]

24 Jack Daw [Eurasian Jackdaw *Corvus monedula*]
Call'd the Chaw with us. It is precarious in its local attachments, the whole flock quitting Cliffs they had long frequented. A tame one made great havoc among some Apples in my garden.

[Jackdaws require sheltered nesting sites to avoid extremes of weather, so favour holes in trees and crevices in buildings, and in coastal and inland rocks, in sufficient quantity to satisfy their gregarious nature. It is generally assumed that this need explains the species' patchy distribution and fluctuating numbers. Birds are omnivorous, but fruit seeds form only a very small percentage of their diet. In the spring of 1858, Couch found Jackdaws building in holes in the elms at Trelawne, "not far from the Rooks" (x, 397), a common association. He had also learned from Harding's study at Trelawne that Jackdaws roosted in the rookery; "some fly daily in that direction from the Cliff station, to which however they also invariably return: & some at least ... appear to be engag'd in incubation" (ix, 140-1). William Minards confirmed this in 1850, assuring Couch "that the party which regularly flies to the Rookery at Trelawny in the evening, & return in the morning are the Males; leaving the females to attend to their Nests thro' the night" (ix, 191). Only the females incubate.

Not only was "chaw" a dialect name for Chough, but also for Jackdaw. Couch himself used Chough in this sense on 13 May 1848: "I am informed that these Birds {Jackdaws} have been seen pulling out the Corn, straw & all, from the mow at Rafel {Raphael, Lansallos}; & flying off to the field, to devour the grain - I afterwards witnessed this myself: the choughs flew in the face of the mow where it had been opened to remove Sheaves for thrashing; & when there were several round Cavities form'd by them or by Pigeons who were numerously engaged in the same plunder. They were all very busy & not at all shy, flying off to the field after short intervals, & again returning" (ix, 145). Couch invariably used "Cornish" Chough when that species was intended.]

Cornish Chough, after Johns

25 Cornish Chough [Red-billed Chough *Pyrrhocorax pyrrhocorax*]
This Bird once frequented the Cliffs in my neighbourhood, but has long since deserted them. I believe it is now only found in the west of Cornwall. [Added later] A few have been seen with us again, 1833.

[In 1831, Couch recorded that at Lizzen, Lansallos, "Three of these birds were seen on the Cliffs ... in the beginning of September; & one was shot" (v, 166), but he had few other records of the "Redlegged Crow". On 30 March 1848, "Wm Minards informs me that a Pair now frequents a Cliff on the back of our hill, not far from Tea Cove. They fly with the Jackdaws, but roost in the next Cove to them: not in the same Cliff". Couch also remarked that the birds pair for life, "but at different times I have known them come to our Cliffs for a short time, & then disappear" (ix, 140-1). By then Choughs were rare on this part of the coast for twenty years or more: "Their numbers are of late much diminished; and in many places where they were formerly common, none are now to be found" (*MNH*, 1830, p. 175). Finally in 1857 (x, 371), Couch reported "A pair came to our Cliffs this Spring; they appear to have formed a nest at or near Lizzon {Lizzen} ground, & now - July - there are five of them - of course three are Young ones".

By 1850, Choughs had become much scarcer in west Cornwall, though records are too few to document the decline. Pairs still frequented The Lizard district when C.A. Johns published *A Week at The Lizard* in 1848, a few still lingering there when F.V. Hill published his Appendix to the 1863 edition. Hill commented that "they are so much sought after, and the eggs so much prized, that they will soon become extinct." Bullmore (1866, pp. 22-3) gave the false impression that birds were then numerous about Falmouth, but the birds taken with baited steel traps came from "Perran sands", hence birds that nested on the cliffs of the north coast about Perranporth; "several dozen of them are sent annually to Falmouth for sale throughout the game season. I have seen as many as five lying dead at one time."

Richard Edmonds (1862, p. 230-31) thought the last breeding pair in the Land's End peninsula was at Tol-Pedn-Penwith, St Levan, having seen four of them in 1849 at nearby Porthgwarra "a few months after they had been taken from a nest in that 'funnel'. I saw them - first, in the little shed wherein they were kept - then flying at large to great distances and returning at the call of their captor as obediently as well-trained falcons." E. H. Rodd knew of them here as well as at Zennor and the cliffs at Trewarvas, Breage (*Pz*, 1850, p. 413), but birds probably nested at Zennor until about 1870. Their last stronghold was on the cliffs from Watergate Bay north to Pentire Glaze, St Minver, with the last known successful breeding in 1947 at four sites, though attempted nesting occurred later. The sole survivor was last seen alive by Anthony Archer-Lock at Beacon Cove, St Mawgan-in-Pydar, on 17 June 1973. Odd birds have turned up since, notably two at Rame Head from 2 August 1986 until January when one was found dead and the other was last seen on the 27th. Although Choughs are considered too sedentary to recolonize Cornwall on their own, hence current attempts to reintroduce birds bred in captivity at Hayle, wild birds appeared at the Lizard in 2001 where they bred successfuly the following year.]

26 Magpie [Black-billed Magpie *Pica pica*]
Maggot, Maggoty-pie. Its singular nest on low trees is known to all.
[By "singular" was probably meant the domed roof which almost all Magpie nests possess. They build at various heights, but on the exposed Cornish coast will do so in low thickets such as blackthorn. Building can start early in the year, as in 1838 when on 6 February Couch found "the foundations laid, weather cold, with smart frost" (vii, 269). April is the usual month for building, as he observed in 1848, noting also that a white one, "with the tail of the ordinary Colour", was paired with a normal bird a little east of Looe (ix, 142). Albino birds have always attracted attention.

Magpie is a contraction of "Magot Pie", first found in Shakespeare's *Macbeth* (Act iii, scene 4), supposedly derived from the French *Margot la pie* because its chattering call was likened to a talkative woman.]

27 Jay [Eurasian Jay *Garrulus glandarius*]
Common about woods. A watchful Bird.

[16-17 September 1848. "These birds for several years have been rather scarce at Trelawny {Trelawne, Pelynt} where formerly they were abundant. But on the above days a large number have arrived - the more strange as Jays are rather solitary" (ix, 152). It is a pity Couch gave no indication of how large a number had been seen. Continental birds occasionally irrupt in mass movements, as in 1979, mainly in October, when 1,250 were reported near St Just-in-Penwith on the 17th, 1000 at Mullion on the 19th, and small numbers elsewhere.]

28 Nutcracker [Spotted Nutcracker *Nucifraga caryocatactes*]
Montagu says it has been shot in Cornwall.

[This is the bird noted by Mr James of St Keverne (*MM*, December 1808, p. 434); "I never saw but one, and that was in the autumn". The year is not stated, but may well have been 1808 because in that year one was shot in north Devon in August. Nutcrackers, principally the Siberian thin-billed race (*N. c. macrorhynchus*), irrupt from time to time in spectacular movements which occasionally reach Britain, though rarely to the far south-west.]

29 Roller [European Roller *Coracias garrulus*]
Pennant mentions one of these rare Birds as having been shot in Cornwall; another was kill'd near Falmouth Octr. 4, 1822.

[The first bird was first recorded by William Borlase ("Additions", *JRIC*, 1865, p. 41): "In the Autumn 1765 on the Moor near Helston ... was shot by Mr Humphry Millett of Ninnis a bird about the bigness of a Dove coloured with a lovely mixture of blue green red and black. ... Having never seen it before, to Mr Brunnick Professor at Copenhagen, I was obliged in October 1766 for the discovery of its name." This was the fourth British record published by Thomas Pennant. The second Cornish occurrence was noted in *MNH*, 1830, p.175. Another was killed "near Penzance" on 8 October 1842 as Couch learned from Clement Jackson (ix, 2, 8). This was a female shot in St Levan and figured in J. T. Blight's *A Week at the Land's End* (1861, p. 155).]

Roller, after Blight

30 Hoopoe [*Upupa epops*]

My friend Mr Jackson observes, three Specimens which have come within his notice were kill'd in April; I have seen two Specimens, kill'd together in Lansallos Parish, & a few beside, one near Looe Sepr. 1834.

Hoopoe, after Bewick

[The Hoopoe has been a regular migrant to Cornwall, chiefly in spring, since Walter Moyle of Bake, St Germans, recorded one shot on 20 April 1720. Couch refers to several Hoopoes, the first at Trelawne, Pelynt: "In a copy of Ray's Synopsis belonging to Sir Harry Trelawny Bart ... One shot in the home meadow a very pretty bird Oct. 1755" (ii, 115). "A fine one shot on 11 April 1833 "in this neighbourhood" (vi, 44). One of those noticed by Jackson was shot on 13 April 1822 and presented to Truro Museum (*WB* 7 vi).

1836: "Mr Coath informs me that the Hoopoe was for several days at his Lisson (Lizzen) home, about Michaelmas. He describes the Bird to me, its size and markings, & recognises it by Bewick's figure: but the Crest differ'd, being formed of only one or two feathers (their length and the length of the bill) & standing quite erect. It would seem that these feathers were moulting. It is strange that several Birds of this species have been seen at & about this place in different years: this makes 4 or 5 within my knowledge ... Wm Minards has known 3 Hoopoes shot at different times at Lizzon, in addition to those already recorded - Strange all at one place" (vii, 149-150).

Another killed on 18 September 1838, "not far from Looe, its stomach stuffed with insects & the skins of Caterpillars" (viii, 16). Another met the same fate in Gorran parish on 6 April 1839 (viii, 30; *WB,* 19 iv). Three were reported in September 1841: Jackson showed him one shot at Pelyn, Lanlivery, the other at Penhale (St Keyne?), while "Mr Coath saw one" at Lizzen, Lansallos, "about the same time" (viii, 220). Another shot "in a meadow on Penhellick" (Pennellick, St Pinnock), 1 May 1844 (viii, 343), met the same depressing fate as one on Windsor Green (probably the place in Lansallos rather than Pelynt), 18 April 1861, and the last Couch recorded "in fine plumage" near Looe on 19 March 1862 (x, 510, 527).]

31 Bee Eater [European Bee-eater *Merops apiaster*]
In the Year 1807 in the Parish of Madron four Birds of this Species were seen, two of which were shot; but the other two escaped. Drew & Hitchens Hist. of Cornwall Vol.1, p585.
[This was the first Cornish record. The second was noted by Couch in his 1838 account: "and from G. S. Borlase, Esqr., {George Simon Borlase FRS, 30 i 1792-19 iii 1837} of Helston, whose decease I lament to see announced while writing this, I have been informed that a flock of twelve came near that Town in 1828; of which eleven were shot". The *West Briton* of 30 May reported that they had been seen the previous week flying over gardens in the vicinity of Helston, and that the birds shot "have been very neatly stuffed by Mr Paull of Helston". G. S. Borlase presented one of the birds to the museum of the Plymouth Athenaeum (E. Moore, 1830, p. 315).]

32 Kingfisher [Common Kingfisher *Alcedo atthis*]
Common. For a note on the nest of this Bird see Loudens Mag. of Nat. Hist. Vol.3. p175. It seems to perform a migration in winter, & hence is sometimes found in unusual situations.
[The note in Louden's *Magazine* (1830) is based on Couch's *Journal* entry for May 1817 (ii, 87): a nest found in a hole at Giggen Cove, Talland, "a quarter of a mile distant from a rivulet; and the nest was thus secured and brought to me. It was composed of dried grass, and lined with hairs and a few feathers. The eggs, three in number, were a little larger than a sparrow's, and of a faint bluish colour, and remarkably transparent". Couch's identification is unlikely, even though nests are occasionally found well away from freshwater and the 1830 account says that the bird "was watched to its nest". Kingfisher's eggs are much larger than a sparrow's, almost spherical, and glossy white like those of other species which nest in holes. Moreover, the nests are not lined, containing only cluttered fish bones. A Wheatear's nest is more plausible.

Couch's "migration in winter" refers to the random dispersal of Kingfishers outside the breeding season when they are frequently seen on the coast. He also wrongly assumed in 1849 that on rivers frequented by the Kingfisher, the Dipper was absent and vice versa (ix, 134).]

33 Water Ouzel [White-throated Dipper *Cinclus cinclus*]

Not uncommon.

[In his *Illustrations of Instinct* (1847, pp. 221-222), Couch published details of a nest in the river bank at Lerryn. It was in a mass of grass and leaves caught in brambles a few inches above the water with the entrance directed towards the bank, so well concealed that it would have gone un-noticed had not a fishing net been cast in and alarmed the bird. The account was given by William Minards "from his own knowledge" in 1834 (vi, 118).

Couch's anthropomorphic idea of birds' intelligence is also illustrated by a Dipper's concealed nest in 1842, "proofs of the intellectual awareness of the Bird" (viii, 260-2), and again in 1847. Birds had bred on the Polperro stream a few years previously, but not in 1847, querying if it was because they "found the situation too disturbed" (ix, 113-4). By 1849, the birds were back and built a nest at the upper Lime Kiln, "where a prop is inserted in the wall, & resting in the mill leat. It is surprising how these Birds could have come into this Nest for a day without being discovered by the Boys who swarm in the neighbourhood, for it is well down in our Town". He graphically described how it entered secretly through the overhanging bushes, and left by rising straight up in the air to the height of Hobb's Hill, "perhaps 300 feet .. from thence to descend or fly diagonally off".

William Minards, who drew his attention to this site, added that he had seen the Dipper catching young eels early on 29 August 1849 in "our River: thus - it extended one wing in the stream, so as to form a Breakwater in the shallow; thus an eddy was created, & when the Eel swam forward to the slack water thus made, the Bird in an instant peck'd it up. He observed this Contrivance several times in different places in the stream: the wing being against the Current. The circumstance of this Bird chusing (*sic*) such a place for the Nest shows that it wish'd to avoid some enemies more dreaded than prying Boys - & that it was quite equal to the task of eluding enquiry of even sharp eyes" (ix, 171-3). Tiny fish form only a small part of the Dipper's diet.]

Cuckows

34 Cuckow [Common Cuckoo *Cuculus canorus*]

The best History of this Bird on the whole is by Dr Jenner, Philosophical Trans. for 1788, which is well abridg'd in an Historical Miscellany of the Curiosities & Rarities in Nature and Art, Vol.1. p139.

Time of the Arrival of the Cuckow in my neighbourhood: (March 23, 1849). April 21, 1816. Apl. 22, 1826. 23rd, 1824, 1832. 24th, 1825. 29th 1823. 30th, 1810, 1828, 1831. May 2, 1813, 1822, (1837). May 9th, 1821. 11th, 1812, 1815. Apl. 19th, 1830. Apl. 25th, 1833, 1836. 27th Apl. 1835. (Dates in brackets are added from Couch's *Journal*.)

Old ones disappear within a few days of each other; they seem to have no local attachments.

[Edward Jenner (1749-1823) of Berkley, Gloucestershire, most famous for his work on vaccination against small-pox, was also a keen naturalist who published his paper on the Cuckoo in the *Philosophical Transactions of the Royal Society* (1788, pp. 219-237). On 19 June 1787, Jenner watched a day-old Cuckoo and a young Dunnock in a nest and saw, to his astonishment, how the former heaved its companion out of the nest. By experiment he proved that the young Cuckoo always removed the eggs of its host in this manner, thus solving a mystery that had long puzzled naturalists.

Couch's last remark shows that Cuckoos normally disappeared from the Polperro area soon after their arrival, which is only to be expected. In Cornwall, Cuckoos mostly lay their eggs in the moorland nests of Meadow Pipits, so that only those that parasitized Rock Pipits' nests lingered on the coast. Thus, on 14 June 1849, "The Crab fishermen, who see most things that pass in the Coves in the morning, inform me, that at this time they observe numerous Cuckoos in the Coves: in companies of 3 or 4 - & in one instance, one of them thought, so many as ten" (ix, 168). Clement Jackson hand-reared Cuckoos from Meadow Pipits' nests and published an account of it and their restlessness at migration time (*TN*, 1851, pp. 175-6). A fully fledged Cuckoo was taken to Couch on 15 June 1835, "from a nest of a Shorelark {Rock Pipit}, as I am informed ... When about to discharge its faeces, while standing in a large cage on straw, it first turn'd completely round, then lifted its posterior high & discharged. It then turned again. This shews its instinct, for there being no nest or elevated rim, all this change of posture & elevation was unnecessary" (vi, 159-160). An older youngster, taken to him on 18 July 1843, proved to be "pugnacious & bites the fingers", but fed itself by 1 August (viii, 307).

Cuckoos resemble predators in flight, as Couch observed on 24 May 1843: "on the wing, flying high like a Hawk; & in this situation actively follow'd by a Crow: - just as we see the Buzzard or Hawk driven & persecuted by a Raven" (viii, 307).

In 1823, Couch found these birds "abounded in an extraordinary degree; so that when riding along the roads, one might be heard in almost every field. In the following year they were as remarkably scarce" (iii, 105; iv, 34; *MNH*, 1830, p.175). A relatively late departure date was 15 October 1828, when Clement Jackson heard one near Morval, "which after being several times repeated seem'd to die away in the distance. He seems to be persuaded it could not have been an imitation by the human voice" (v, 49-50). Confirmed sightings in December are known in England.

His first observation, other than arrival date, was on 17 June 1821 (iii, 111) when "Riding in a woody brake I saw five Cuckows in Company, but apparently on no very good terms. I observe this is a very shy bird, carefully avoiding to fly over where I was, tho' smaller birds did it freely. Perhaps these were males courting one female - query - is it the male or the female that utters the common sound, & why are so many males requir'd to one female?" Lack of "local attachments" was prompted in 1827: "Tho' I have been as usual about the County, I have not heard one of these birds for the season. Yet I have been informed that they have been in plenty in the west. This shews that they have no local attachments, like the Swallow" (v, 17).

A quaint story, told to him by Frank Coath in April 1832, "which he says he saw himself", concerned Mr Moon, a barber in Liskeard, who "once found a Young Cuckow, & brought it to his house; where it attracted the attention of several Canaries in an extraordinary manner. These Birds, being loose, fluttered about the Cuckow's Cage, & being suffered to enter it, began to feed it; & the Cuckow would suffer itself to be fed by no other. This continued for some time, & multitudes of people went to see it" (vi, 11-12). Just as odd is William Laughrin's story of a Cuckoo he saw on 14 June 1861 on the road playing with a Field Mouse: "not like that of a bird of prey with a Captive, but real play - the mouse appearing to play as well as the bird - & equally unwilling to give it up. When he was seen the mouse ran into the hedge - but presently came out again to his playmate. The Cuckoo then flew on to some distance - but shew'd much unwillingness to leave the place" (x, 513-4).]

35 Uncertain Species [Yellow-billed Cuckoo *Coccyzus americanus*]
In the Year 1813 a singular Bird, nearly white, was taken up in a very exhausted state near Stratton. It was rather larger than the thrush, & resembled the Cuckow Species. It had long feathers reaching from its thighs to the extremities of its feet: Drew's Hist. of Cornwall Vol.1 p585. What Species, or even genus this was, must remain matter of doubt, & whether a straggler or escap'd from a Cage.

[Added later] Perhaps this was the Virginian Cuckow (Eyton's Rarer Birds p23) of which a few have been taken in Britain.

[Couch published the record in his 1838 account, without the date, under its alternative name of Carolina Cuckoo. This was the first British record. C. S. Gilbert (1817, p. 318) adds that the bird "was preserved by the Rev. John King, of Stratton, and presented by him to the President of the

Yellow-billed Cuckoo, after Eyton

Royal Society, who has deposited it in Mr Bullock's Museum, in Piccadilly". William Bullock was a traveller and naturalist, famous, or rather infamous, for hunting down one of the last Great Auks in the Orkney Isles off Papa Westray in 1812. He failed then, but acquired the bird in the following year and exhibited it in his collection in the London Museum of Natural History which he opened at 22 Piccadilly in 1809 and soon afterwards in the Egyptian Hall nearby. His huge collection of curiosities was a great attraction until sold in May 1819. Many of the stuffed birds (over 3,000 of them) were bought by Lord Derby who founded the Derby Museum in Liverpool, but the "Nondescript cuckoo", Lot 52 on 5 May, was sold to Dr Leach of the British Museum for £3.3.0. The bird does not survive in the Sub-dept. of Ornithology at Tring, and its ultimate fate is not known. William Elford Leach (1790-1836) was born in Plymouth and the man in whose honour Leach's Storm-petrel was named by C. J. Temminck in 1820.]

Woodpeckers
36 Green Woodpecker [*Picus viridis*]

Not uncommon.
[In 1858, Couch reported that "For more than 30 Years I have seen or heard a pair of green Woodpeckers having nested in the old chestnut trees which stand in the field leading from Trelawny [Trelawne] House to the Garden" (x, 399-402). He knew of only two nest holes there and described the larger one and its contents in great detail, making a sketch of it and two addled eggs which he inserted in his "own copy of Mr Yarrell's Birds". The following April he found the nest occupied by Jackdaws; "we shall see what the poor Woodpeckers will resort to next", though he never made known the outcome (x, 402-3, 438). A full report dated 28 December 1858 was published in the *Zoologist* for 1859, as

well as in 1860 a note about the Jackdaws and the following record of the only other nest site Couch was aware of. In 1860, Stephen Clogg told him "that last year this bird made its nest - I believe for the first time - in a pollard ash at Killmanorth {Kilminorth, Talland}, not far from the farmhouse ... but the place is much more exposed to passers by than at Trelawny" (x, 460).

Like the Great Spotted Woodpecker, the Green was formerly rare in west Cornwall. Writing on 4 March 1873, E. H. Rodd noted that "only one or two examples, over a period of nearly half a century" had come to his notice in the Land's End district. Increasing numbers were being reported in the Truro area with seven seen together at Bosvigo, according to a paragraph he read in a daily paper. All three woodpeckers, more common in east Cornwall, were then breeding annually on the Trebartha estate in North Hill (*JRIC*, 1873, p. 161)]

37 Greater Spotted Woodpecker [Great Spotted Woodpecker *Dendrocopos major*]
In a Copy of Ray's Syn. Av. is a Note "A male one of this Sort taken alive out of a hollow tree Dec. 1755" at Trelawny. [Added later] One killed near Liskeard January 1834 [*J*, vi, 77].
[The 1755 record from Trelawne, Pelynt, was written in John Ray's *Synopsis Avium et Piscium*, completed by 29 February 1694 and published pothumously in 1713. It is the first Cornish record. In 1838, Couch noted that "This bird is rare with us; & the few that have been seen, are only in winter" (viii, 21). The Liskeard bird was a female. The species was particularly scarce in west Cornwall until a westward expansion began in about 1870, although Rodd knew of one killed at Mayon, Sennen, before 1838 (*RRIC*, 1838, p. 40).]

38 Little Woodpecker [Lesser Spotted Woodpecker *Dendrocopos minor*]
A specimen kill'd near Liskeard Sep 29, 1831 - a male in moult, weight 10 drams.
[The above specimen, "not bigger than a Sparrow", was in Clement Jackson's collection (v, 166). This secretive species remains very scarce in Cornwall, its status unlikely to have changed since Couch's day. His record is the first for the County. In 1816 he was aware of two resident species; "pubsecens - little woodpecker - viridis - green woodpecker" (i, 121), but there is no evidence that he had seen the former at that date.]

39 Nuthatch [Wood Nuthatch *Sitta europaea*]
It is rare in Cornwall [Added later], but I have seen several Specimens; and near Boconnock I am informed it is not exceedingly rare. One active at Trelawny [Trelawne, Pelynt], Feby. 7, 1842.

[His earliest record is in 1829 when Clement Jackson received one on 28 February "from Cornwall" (v, 63). The Nuthatch is certainly scarcer in Cornwall than further east and was apparently rarer in the 19th century than nowadays, particularly in west Cornwall. Couch's statement is, nevertheless, too pesimistic. His 1838 published comment is nearer the truth: "Local; but not uncommon in some situations; as near Liskeard, and at Boconnoc". In 1858 (x, 402), Couch noted that the nest of this species, like that of the Green Woodpecker, "is also in the trunk of a Chestnut tree - in Trelawny Garden".]

40 Wryneck [Eurasian Wryneck *Jynx torquilla*]

I do not think this is a very rare, so much as from its habits, it is an unobserved Bird. One was taken near Falmouth April 1825.

[This is a scarce but regular passage migrant in Cornwall. As a breeding bird it has declined with no British record since 1989. In Couch's day it may well have nested in parkland and orchards to the east of Bodmin Moor, as implied by the Revd T. Johnes in Mrs Bray's *The Borders of the Tamar and Tavy* (1836, p. 304). Couch makes no mention of the Wryneck in his *Journal*.]

Thrushes

41 Missel Thrush [Mistle Thrush *Turdus viscivorus*]

Resides with us winter & summer, but tho' common, never abounds. [Added later] See Journal 1835, vol.6. The largest song Bird.

[The reference to the "Holm Thrush" is for 1833 (vi, 50): "As some doubt has been thrown on the singing of this Bird, I record that Richard Batten informs me, when he was in Bodmin Prison, a nest of young Holm Thrushes was brought in, one of which he rear'd; & its Song was so beautiful as to attract the notice of visitors, & procur'd him the offer of 10 shillings for the Bird". What doubt there was about its song is unclear, being so well known that its song in stormy weather gave rise to dialect Storm-cock.

In March 1837, Couch was astonished to see nine birds togther, rather than the usual "several" in a tree at Trelawne (vii, 176), while in October 1834, William Minards counted two flocks of 22 and 23 birds "at no great distance from each other" (vii, 26-27). Family parties and small flocks are not unusual in autumn and early winter, though Minards' birds could have been migrants, north British birds being partially so. J. Hocken of Penhillick, St Pinnock, told Couch that in the summer of 1837, "when the Black Caterpillar in myriads was devouring his Turnips, these Birds assembled in one field by hundreds, he never saw so many together before - & they devour'd these caterpillars so as to save the Turnips, whilst those of most of his neighbours were destroy'd" (vii, 270). This may be a case of mistaken identity; the largest authenticated British flock comprised 280 flying west on 12 September 1954 at Limpsfield Common in Surrey (E. Simms, 1978, *British Thrushes*, p. 199). Simms also noted (p. 112) that migrant Fieldfares have "a strong liking for turnips". Whatever the species of bird, the black caterpillars were larvae of the Turnip Sawfly *Athalia spinarum*. The largest recorded invasion caused massive devastation in 1835 in southern counties and to a lesser extent in the following few years, devouring leaves in whole fields "in the course of a few days" (Eleanor A. Ormerod, 1890, *A Manual of Injurious Insects*, pp. 194-5).

Mistle Thrushes are early nesters, and in 1836 Couch described in detail a nest "as large as a Boy's hat" built only four feet above the ground in a fork of a pear tree in his garden, noting that where the space between the branches was wider, the birds had strengthened the nest with "a firm layer of Clay around the edge, & nowhere else". The birds allowed him to approach to 10 feet from the tree; any closer and he was "saluted with the most violent alarm" and dive-bombed within a few feet "in a manner that I can readily imagine would have terrified any small Animal, or even a Child" (vii, 80-81, 83). In 1838, J. Hocken told Couch that Mistle Thrushes bred "abundantly" at Penhillick, but for a year or two had suffered "by having their young in the nest devoured by Crows" (vii, 270).

One need not question Mr Hocken's truthfulness, but what does one make of the tale told to Clement Jackson in 1837 by Mr Pengelly of East Looe? - "a person of veracity, & himself an observer & bird fancier. Not far from each other on a tree at St Martin's {-by-Looe}, were the Nests of a Missel Thrush & Chaffinch: the former with young, the latter with eggs. When the former bird approach'd the nest with food to supply the young, the Chaffinch left her nest, went to the Missel thrush, prevail'd on it to let her have the food, & went & fed the young Missels with it" (vii, 222).]

42 Fieldfare [*Turdus pilaris*]

Seldom arrives before December, & keeps in fields in loose flocks. In 1832 they were here in April, & again within the first ten days of September.

[On 23 December 1815, Couch observed the first for the winter, how "They keep in flocks, in the fields on high ground, & seem not to wander far from the places they like ... They are not found near places of water, like thrushes, nor in the sides of hedges, but on the plain grassy field; & where feeding in a flock, single Birds often rise, fly a little way, & then alight, by which means the whole flock goes on" (i, 83). Even in severe weather on 23 January 1823 the species "scarcely ever wanders into the garden, where the others {thrushes} frequent, altho' it is as much weakened & tam'd as any of them" (iii, 155).]

43 Blackbird [Common Blackbird *Turdus merula*]

Pied Specimens are not uncommon; a young one perfectly white was taken from the nest near St Austell June 1829.

[The pied bird was fully fledged taken from the nest and in the possession of Clement Jackson (v, 67). One of his first observations is of a Blackbird in song on 19 February 1816 (i, 102), not unusual at that time of year.

More interesting is his observation on winter feeding on 23 January 1823 (iii, 155): "The weather is now very severe, the snow for several days covering the ground, & being hard frozen, I observe of the Genus Turdus that altho' they are now suffering severely from cold & hunger, the blackbird & redwing are very particular in taking their food. The latter bird is very tame; yet both these pull & beat their prey very much before they devour it; whereas the Thrush does not so much so, by which means it is much more frequently taken on the pin and thread than the others." In autumn 1869, Couch noted that Blackbirds, but not thrushes, "are now devouring my pears" (xii 184). Windfalls of soft fruit are a common feast for all thrushes, though pears apparently rarely with Song Thrushes.

Always interested in migrating birds, Couch noted on 30 October 1833 that "A blackbird flew on board a fishing Boat at a good distance from land ... a fine day. It perhaps was crossing the Channel since there has been little wind to blow it off for a day or two" (vi, 72).]

Blackbird, after Bewick

In 1835, Yarrell told Couch that the house in the background of the Blackbird was Bewick's birthplace - Cherry-burn House near Eltringham in Northumberland.

44 Ring Ouzel [*Turdus torquatus*]

Scarce.

[This scarce passage migrant nested on Bodmin Moor in the 1840s, but rarely in the 20th century. Nicholas Hare saw eight birds at the Cheesewring, St Cleer, on 31 May 1843 (*RCPS*, 1846, p. 28). He found a nest with four eggs near there in 1847, and three more nests in 1848 (*Pz*. 1848, p. 212). E. H. Rodd had also noted "young, scarcely fledged" on the moors near North Hill, "viz.- Hawk's Tor, Kilmar &c" (*Pz*, 1850, p. 405-6).

Couch's first record is of one seen in late November 1826 at Looe (iv, 155). A pair of migrants were at Bodinnick for a few days up to 1 April 1833, and another shot at Lansallos, 20 April 1842 (vi, 48; viii, 259). One on the point of "emigrating" was killed on the seaward side "of our Hill" on 22 September 1845, and another seen on the 15th in 1848 (ix, 53, 152). These records suggest the species was rather more common then than now. Winter records are rare, but Couch had one in his garden on 22 January 1862 (x, 525).]

45 Thrush [Song Thrush *Turdus philomelos*]

Common.

[December 1836. "We had two days of frost, followed on the 26th by a fall of snow, of a fine dusty sort - wind NE, & these birds, especially the thrushes, abound, countless thousands: they must have come from far, driven by the wind, for our neighbourhood could not have contain'd a thousand part of the thrushes now swarming. They are much tam'd, tho' no past weather here will explain how. Blackbirds are but little increas'd - Redwings common - but the swarms are mostly thrushes - which must have arriv'd here in the night, for they were not here yesterday. Numbers also have been passing westward. All gone by the next morning, except our own old Birds" (vii, 154-5).

Song Thrushes occasionally nest on the ground, as found by William Minards in April 1844: "built on the ground, & somewhat in it, in the middle of a turnip field, shaded only by the leaves of the turnips; the outside structure form'd of portions of dried turnip leaves; the inside lin'd with the usual mortar, & with 4 eggs. The nest is somewhat deeper than usual, & a little bent in at the top; eggs pale blue, with small dark spots, like points, at the larger end" (viii, 343).]

46 Redwing [*Turdus iliacus*]

It comes regularly in winter, & is at first very shy, keeping in high ground; it is much and quickly tamed by cold weather.

[The *Journal* records consist of arrival dates and flocks in winter. Typical is that of February 1818: "We have had a pretty copious fall of snow; & when it was yet falling, large flocks of birds, in endless succession were flying towards the West, the way from which the snow came. They were Larks, Starlings, Redwings, Fieldfares, & I believe Holm Thrushes, Linnets & Chaffinches, each in flocks. The Redwing, tho' a shy bird, feels the cold extremely sensibly & soon. It seem'd to be most disabled of any" (ii, 119-120).]

47 Golden Oriole [Eurasian Golden Oriole *Oriolus oriolus*]

A male Specimen was taken near St Austell March 1824; & a female was taken by a fisherman of Polperro May 3, 1828.

[Mr James of St Keverne knew of two records before 1808, but the St Austell capture is the first dated occurrence for the County. The 1828 bird, a female, "Golden Thrush" had been caught at sea, "just starv'd to death" (v, 31). It was probably a female that pitched on the yard of Mr Puckey's boat "when about four leagues off" on 25 May 1831, although the fisherman declared the bird to be as large as a pigeon. Similarly, in May 1835 a female was taken "last week" on board a fishing boat near the Lizard (*WB*, 29 v). Birds occasionally remain late in the autumn: Lieut. C. Walcott saw a female somewhere in Cornwall on 2 November 1854, but had no need to shoot it because he was familiar with the species in Greece and Italy (x, 210). Sightings later in the year are known from elsewhere in southern England.

Golden Orioles remain scarce regular migrants, but have never been known to nest in Cornwall. J. C. Bellamy (1839, p. 201) said it was occasionally obtained in wooded districts in summer, as at Mount Edgcumbe (formerly part of Devon), but this is no proof of breeding. An emaciated but brilliantly plumaged male captured at Trevider Moor, bordering St. Buryan and Paul parishes, was given to Rodd on 1 May 1859 (*Z*, letter dated 2 May; *RRIC*, 1859, p. 20), and is the bird illustrated by J.T. Blight (1861, p. 54) who wrongly dated it to the following year and gave the locality as Trevelloe, less than a mile from Trevider.]

Golden Oriole, after Blight

48 Chatterer [Bohemian Waxwing *Bombycilla garrulus*]

A specimen was shot at Restormel in January 1829 [*J*, v, 63].

[The Bohemian Waxen Chatterer, as it was formerly called, is a regular winter visitor to eastern England, but rarely reaches so far south west as Cornwall. One was shot near Pennance Point, Budock, in the winter of 1847 (*TN* 1851, p. 64). One of the largest invasions was in 1849-1850 when one was shot at Trereiffe, Madron, in mid-January, a second was captured alive at Roundwood, Feock, and another shot at Bodmin about the same time (*RCG*, 1 ii 1850). Couch saw at Clement Jackson's a specimen shot near Lostwithiel on 15 January 1850 (ix, 182).]

49 Starling [Common Starling *Sturnus vulgaris*]

It visits us in flocks in winter, arriving in September or October, but I believe never breeds here. It associates with Rooks & is very restless when seeking food. I have not seen for many years such immense flocks as were common many years since.

[Mr James of St Keverne (1808, p. 434) noted that "some few breed in the cliffs", presumably in the Lizard peninsula. Couch evidently heard of other breeding records because, in his 1838 account, he noted nesting in "the Cliffs on the North East of the County". Even so, regular nesting did not spread into Cornwall until about the 1850s. The first recorded was at Trewardale, Blisland: "in the spring of 1855 ... a pair built in an abandoned woodpecker's nest, and from that pair ... a considerable colony has now established itself among the rooks here, and several pairs breed annually, and are spreading to other places in the parish" (Sir John Maclean, 1873, *The Parochial and Family History of the Deanery of Trigg Minor*, Vol.1, p. 64). Couch's notes, therefore, concern the arrival of autumn flocks, such as that first seen on 22 October 1815 (i, 65), or the young Starling that "flew on board a fishing boat at 3 or 4 leagues from land" on 24 October 1845, thus proving its migration (ix, 61).]

The word Thrush is descriptive of the spotted plumage of these Birds, as is Turdus in Latin; the latter word has also been applied to the wrass[e], for the same reason.

[Thrush derives from Old English *thrysce*, Middle English *thrushe*, a variant of *throstle*, *throstel*. Latin *turdus* simply means thrush and a species of fish, and nothing to do with spotted, in Latin *maculosus*.]

Grosbills

50 Hawfinch [*Coccothraustes coccothraustes*]

A male Specimen was kill'd near Looe Novr. 4, 1828, & another escap'd. It is understood that others had been seen.

["A workman said Birds like these were in the same place last year, and that in April 1828, 2 Grossbeaks killed near St Austle by Mr Lakes" (v, 53; vi, 44). The Hawfinch is a rare and unpredictable visitor to Cornwall, Rodd reporting "numerous flights" in the West Penwith area since August 1838 (*RRIC*, 1838, p. 40). It could turn up at almost any time of year. Clement Jackson obtained one from Tideford, St Germans, on 15 January 1842, while another was shot near Looe "a few weeks before" (viii, 240). In about January 1855, one was shot in Venslooe Wood, Pelynt (x, 215; *RCG*, 26 i 1855).]

51 Bullfinch [Common Bullfinch *Pyrrhula pyrrhula*]

With us it is call'd the Hoop or golden Hoop. In January & February it is common in gardens, where it is very destructive to the buds of gooseberry bushes. [Added later] It very rarely breeds with us.

[On 27 January 1816, Couch "kill'd some Bullfinches, which were devouring the Buds of the gooseberry; & find their gizzards to be stuff'd with the buds in a triturated state. I have no doubt that the object of their search is the bud, & not worms in the bud. These birds are now in plenty" (i, 96). By May (ii, 3), Couch found that "After the time that the Bullfinches did so much harm in gardens, in the beginning of Spring, I have not seen one, tho' I have been in different parts of the Country: the places to which they retire to breed, must therefore be extremely private." All his records are for the winter months when they plundered his gooseberries, as on 10 January 1817 and 1 February 1848 (ii, 67; ix, 139).]

52 Crossbill [Common Crossbill *Loxia curvirostra*]

Crossbill, after Bewick

Figure in Bewick's Br. Birds Vol.1 p.154, but in a specimen in my possession the points of the bill cross'd each other more than in this figure. I kept a Crossbill in a Cage for several months, it was brought from France in a fir-cage, which it nearly tore to pieces, I suppose on account of the turpentine; for it did no injury to an oaken Cage. In its manners it much resembled a Parrot, drawing itself about the roof of the cage, often with the back downward, by means of its bill. It had a sweet but low Song, which was heard only when the Bird was in solitude; if any one were in the room, it ceas'd. When devouring seeds, both mandibles were brought together, the colours were continually changing; but the fine pink and crimson tints, when once lost, were never recover'd.

Couch's watercolour of the Crossbill

[The watercolour drawing is of the French bird which Couch kept from November 1821 until its death on 4 May 1822 (iii, 126, 133, 139). It was brought with two others from St Pol-de-Leon "and were very tame to take". In his 1838 account, Couch described the Crossbill as "An irregular visitant in small companies". In 1835, the Revd J. Lakes killed several "this week" near St Austell and sent them to Clement Jackson on 17 September (vii, 19). On 30 June 1837, a migrant "flew on board a fishing Boat, about 4 leagues from Land" (vii, 219), while the following year, Jackson had another "kill'd Sepr. 24 somewhere a little west from us" (viii, 16). Crossbills can turn up at almost any time, with records dating back to Carew's famous description of them as "an over-familiar harme", probably during the well documented invasion of 1593.]

53 Greenfinch [European Greenfinch *Carduelis chloris*]
Common, but not abundant.
[Numbers can vary greatly, the species suffering in severe winters. Couch followed Bewick in placing this finch with the grosbeaks. All, of course, are finches as Couch recognised in his published 1838 account. He added it to his Cornish list on 16 November 1816 and described the plumage of one in January 1820 (ii, 62; iii, 54-5).]

54 Uncertain Species [Two-barred Crossbill *Loxia leucoptera*]
In this place I arrange a Bird of which I receiv'd the following account from one of our fishermen. He discover'd it when at Sea, attach'd to the quarter of a vessel which he went on board of that was coming up the Channel; but the Captain had not seen it before he pointed it out. It was confin'd in the binnacle for me, but unfortunately it afterwards made its escape. He described it as about the size of a Sparrow but the body rather longer, head round, bill small & strong. Colours beautiful & various, much like those of some of the Moth kind, & very soft to the feeling; back red with some stripes of white across (I believe the wings). Quere - Is this the *Loxia falcirostra*? a Species of North America, that has been taken in Britain.
[This undated account, not published by Couch in 1838, fits the Two-barred Crossbill, a species that breeds in northern pine forests on both sides of the Atlantic, though most British examples are undoubtedly of European origin. See also under **234** below.]

Finches
55 Goldfinch [European Goldfinch *Carduelis carduelis*]
Common.
[All Couch's records up to 1817 comprise dates of singing, while a series from 1846 to 1851 deals with times of appearance at Polperro. Thus, from about 7 March 1846 appeared "The first since the autumn ... and at the end of the second week they are by hundreds: - more than our usual numbers. It seems therefore that some of them are in passage to some other stations" (ix 73-4). Not all British Goldfinches are resident and many ringing recoveries have been made in France and Iberia (I. Newton, 1972, *Finches*, pp. 39-40), but continental birds also pass through Britain. Autumn flocks are generally larger than those in spring. Most of Couch's records are at these times or in winter, as in January 1850 during severe frost "with snow thro' the greater part of the County, altho' not here, a few pairs

of these Birds appear'd. None had been seen for a long time before" (ix, 182). Winter 1857-8 was generally mild and "little families of these birds have come about at intervals, & in the first half of February, a considerable flock was seen near Trelawny. It appears therefore that they have been less migratory this season than usual - but still wandering much" (x, 393).

In autumn 1869, Couch noted that this bird "was formerly exceedingly common & often seen in our gardens. It usually left us in Winter, but returned in Spring, & even a few in winter when snow fell or frost came. But I did not see one last Winter, nor thro' this Summer, nor as I believe, thro' the Summer before this last. Yet our hedges and shelter has not been altered - it is even increased. My garden seemed formerly a favourite resort with an occasional nest for this & other small birds; but not so for several years past. Whether this applies to our other small birds I scarcely know, but the Robin was formerly more frequently, & the Bullfinch did not plunder my gooseberry buds last Spring" (xii, 184).]

56 Chaffinch [*Fringilla coelebs*]

Common, always single, & without any peculiarity of habit, as reported in some places. Here called Copperfinch.

[These remarks are not repeated in his 1838 account other than "common". "Single" is inappropriate for a species which habitually flocks outside the breeding season. In Britain large flocks are of migrants from the Continent. Most of his references are to dates of singing, but noted on 27 May 1817 how they fed eagerly on the leaves of black currents and gooseberries covered with aphids (ii, 85). Birds commonly peck at their reflection in windows, assuming it to be a rival bird, as Lewis Harding found at Trelawne in April 1854 (x, 188). Copper Finch was dialect in Devon and Cornwall. Couch noted the name in 1817 (ii, 68).]

57 Mountainfinch [Brambling *Fringilla montifringilla*]

Rare, & in winter only.

[The first was reported by Couch in 1816: "W. Stephens informs me that the Mountain finch was once caught at Looe, in severe cold weather" (ii, 20). One, which had been shot, was taken to Couch on 1 February 1823 (iii, 157). About December 1852, Clement Jackson told him that "many ... have been seen in the wood at Polvellyn {Polvellan, West Looe} for a few days. He has obtained 6 Specimens" (x, 98). On 2 October 1857 (x, 381) "in a ride towards Looe - near Wayland, I saw a few of those birds, in Company with some Linnets - feeding on Seeds. I note it because of the earliness of the Season."]

58 Linnet [Common Linnet *Carduelis cannabina*]
Common.

[Couch gives this the scientific name *Fringilla linota* formerly assumed to be a distinct species, but in reality only the young of the Linnet or "Greater Redpole" *F. cannabina* as he called it. His early references, mostly in 1816, are to dates of singing or flocking, and congregating "in large numbers" on 15 September 1820 (iii, 83). Autumn and winter flocks of over a thousand have been recorded in Cornwall. See next entry.]

59 Greater Redpole [Common Linnet *Carduelis cannabina*]
Not common.

[In view of his brief comment in the previous entry, "Not common" is nonsense. Couch was afterwards aware of the confusion over identification, and in his 1838 account he only refers to the Linnet, without comment on its abundance. He added that the "Lesser Redpole" {Redpoll} was a distinct species but did not know if it "be found in Cornwall". The latter, a British form of the Common Redpoll *C. flammea*, was first identified in Cornwall by W. P. Cocks in fields near Pennance, Budock, sometime before 1849 under the name *Linaria canescens* (*RCPS*, 1849, p. 43).]

60 Sparrow [House Sparrow *Passer domesticus*]
Common.

[Couch makes a few references in his *Journals* to tree nests, now rarely, if ever, reported in Cornwall though still constructed on the Isles of Scilly. After the hard frost in January 1987 that destroyed many of the *Pittosporum* hedges, a good number of these nests, like miniature rookeries, were very noticeable on St Martin's.

In 1831, Mr Coath of Raphael, Lansallos, gave "rewards to the Apprentices for as many eggs of Sparrows as could be obtained: in consequence of which all the Nests of these Birds that could be discover'd, have been repeatedly robb'd. At last, finding all their efforts to raise a brood ineffectual, the Birds have left building in the holes of the houses, where hitherto their nests had always been placed; & have all of them built their nests in the trees near the Townplace. The nests are large, chiefly form'd of feathers, loosely fasten'd together; but are placed where the leaves are thickest" (v, 156-157). Mr Coath's exercise was predicatably fruitless. In 1835, three House Sparrows at Raphael commandeered the nests of House Martins, "enlarg'd the opening & brought their own straw for the nests: one of them, in order to do this, cast out the young Martins, just beginning to get feathers: they were yet alive when I found them beneath the nest, & yet the Sparrows' nest in their lost place was apparently built" (vi, 158-159). Also in 1835, "A Sparrow's nest {was found} close at the side of the nest of a Rook at Trelawny", Pelynt (vi, 153).

The sparrow's close association with man attracted Couch's early attention: 22 January 1816, "It is curious to observe the characters of these Sparrows. Dwelling near to Man without trusting him, they have occasion to put in practice all the vigilance ... they are masters of ... You may pass near them without disturbing them, but immediately as any attention is directed towards them, they are off, & it is extremely difficult to take them in a snare" (i, 92-3).

A most extraordinary account was given by Couch in January 1835 (vi, 129): "The Sparrows devour Cockchafers, and I know that they destroy young Pigeons by pecking thro' the Crop and devouring the Corn that is in it. The wound is never suffer'd to heal, because they come often to devour the soften'd grain."]

61 Black Cap [Blackcap *Sylvia atricapilla*]

Rare in my immediate neighbourhood; but I am inform'd that it is common near St Austle. This should be class'd with the warblers; but is not arrang'd with them for want of room.

[The Blackcap was more locally distributed than nowadays. Its rarity about Polperro is not surprising considering the lack of trees in Lewis Harding's photographs of Polperro in the 1860s. Blackcaps were known to occur "in the winter months sparingly in sheltered spots in the neighbourhood of Penzance" (E. H. Rodd, 1880, p. 38). The wintering habit has increased greatly in Britain, particularly in suburban gardens and similar habitats in the south and west since the 1960s; these birds are not British bred but continental immigrants.]

Buntings
62 Common Bunting [Corn Bunting *Miliaria calandra*]

Common.

[In June 1816, Couch wrote "I think the Bunting is common with us (Emberiza miliaris) sitting at this time on a Bush or low tree by the wayside, and singing a short & not very pleasing song" (ii, 20). E. H. Rodd called it "generally distributed: frequents open and enclosed ground, and may be observed in nearly every hedge-row" (*Pz*, 1850, p. 411). This resident species has declined considerably nationally since the 1960s. In Cornwall it maintains a much depleted population on parts of the north coast west from St Minver.]

63 Yellowhammer [*Emberiza citrinella*]

Common. With us call'd the Gladdy.

[Couch wrote in 1815 that "The yellowhammer remains with us all the Winter, commonly, but I think in severe seasons it goes away, since I saw none during the severe snow, two years since, tho' I think if there had been any in the neighbourhood I should have seen them. They cannot however go far since at that time, as soon as the weather became mild, some were seen. Perhaps they go only to the west part of the County" (i, 85). He first noted young on 29 June 1816 (ii, 24). In severe winter weather, Yellowhammers tended to congregate around farms. The species is now much rarer than formerly. "Gladdy", dialect in Cornwall and Devon, derives from Anglo-Saxon *gladde* (bright).]

64 Cirl [Cirl Bunting *Emberiza cirlus*]

This Bird is common, & not migrant.

[Couch includes a thumbnail sketch of the male. The species had only been discovered as a British resident by Col. George Montagu in 1800 at Kingsbridge in south Devon. Some have suggested that this species, more at home in more southerly latitudes, had only recently colonised Britain, but there is no proof of this and no evidence of migration from the Continent. It is far more likely that the Cirl Bunting had been overlooked until then. Henry Mewburn of St Germans sent a specimen, shot in 1822 by John Drew (of Devonport) at Ford in Stoke Damerel, Devon, to Thomas Bewick who figured it in the 6th edition (1826) of his *British Birds*. Mewburn "has besides ascertained that they breed in the neighbourhood, frequenting woods and high trees, and like the Common Bunting, generally perched near the top".

Early in 1826, Couch noted that Clement Jackson had found the nest of the Cirl Bunting, presumably in 1825, in a hedge "along the lane near Liskeard" (iv, 129-30). "The female sprung out of the hedge, dropp'd to the ground, fluttering along as if unable to fly" and was soon joined by the male which acted likewise. Searching the hedge, Jackson found the nest with three eggs, one a "dusky white with feint red stripes, the others had scarcely any stripes." On a ride of five miles on 20 April 1829, Couch saw two pairs; "The note of the male is monotonous, but often repeated. They are not shy and must be numerous" (v, 64-5). On 21 March 1849, he noted that "I have not seen one for a considerable time - of course the Birds which keep near us in Summer must be migrated, but today I have seen three very fine males within a short distance. They have therefore now returned" (ix, 160). Numbers have always fluctuated. The breeding population is now virtually confined to south Devon and is probably extinct in Cornwall except as a non-breeding visitor.

Cirl Bunting, after Bewick

Riding over the high ground at Killigarth, Talland, on 30 March 1821, Couch saw, "perch'd on an elevated spray", a bird he believed to be "the Oenanthe altera of Aldrovandus" (Ulisses Aldrovanni, 1522-1605) and gave the Latin description in Ray's *Synopsis* (iii, 101). It appears in English in Ray, 1678 (p. 233): "*Aldrovandus* hath another *Oenanthe*, which is a little less than the former {Wheatear}, but yet bigger than a *Sparrow*, on the Head, Neck, Back, and lesser Wing-feathers of a reddish yellow, deeper on the Back, lighter on the Breast, having black Eyes, behind which is also a long black spot, of a semilunar figure: A long, slender, black Bill; black Wing-feathers, whose ends are a yellow, as are also those of the Tail-feathers." This does not fit anything accurately and is certainly not closely related to one of the wheatears. Aldrovandus was not famed for accuracy. Couch noted that the yellow was bright, and "the black, particularly the black line over the eye, intense". He queried if it might be the Cirl Bunting, a bird it more closely resembles - excluding the long, slender bill - than any other small bird he might have encountered.]

65 Reedbunting [Reed Bunting *Emberiza schoeniclus*]

[Couch makes no comment and in his 1838 account only calls it "local", which it still is as a breeding bird at such localities as Marazion Marsh and Par beach pool. Like other buntings it has become much rarer since the 1960s.]

66 Uncertain Species [Ortolan Bunting *Emberiza hortulana*]

On the 6th of May 1828 a Bird was seen in Killigarth Warren [Talland], of the following Description, as given me by one who saw it, & had good opportunity of noting it; for the Bird was not shy. It was rather less than the Hedge Sparrow, &

appear'd rather short on its legs; a fine eye, fine green on the throat & round the eyes to the back; back & tail covers red, wings dark, reddish legs. It perch'd on the stalk of foxglove. I have suppos'd it to be the Greenheaded Bunting, E. Chlorocephala Lin, of which there is a figure in Bewick's Addenda to Br. Birds (vol 2) p 1.

Ortolan Bunting, after Bewick

[Couch did not include this species in his published 1838 account, perhaps because he doubted the identification. The Ortolan is somewhat larger than a Hedge Sparrow (though size is difficult to estimate in the field), but an olive-green head and chest are diagnostic of the male. Spring records of this rare passage migrant are uncommon, most being recorded in September and October. If correct, this is by far the earliest Cornish record, the first confirmed bird having been shot on a wall in Tresco Abbey, Scilly, on 7 October 1851 (x, 33; Clark & Rodd, 1906, p.11).]

67 Snowflake [Snow Bunting *Plectrophenax nivalis*]
The Cornwall Gazette of the 14th of October 1818 reports, that Mr [Joseph] Hoskin, of Cubert, shot one Specimen, out of a flock of about an hundred, a week before that date [*J*, iii, 1.]
[The Hoskin family lived at Ellenglaze, Cubert. The cliff-tops here are, to this day, among the most likely spots to see these autumn migrants and occasional wintering birds. In his 1844 Supplement, Couch noted that the species had "been shot near Penzance, and I believe at other places in the county". The Penzance bird was shot by Mr Jenkins in the winter of 1843 (viii, 297). Several in "variegated plumage" were taken in west Cornwall in 1845 (ix 57-8). Rodd earlier noted that one had been killed at Paul, a few miles west of Penzance, "and others seen by myself on Carn Galver", Zennor (*RRIC*, 1838, p. 40). Birds were rarely seen in the Polperro area; Couch had one taken to him on 15 March 1852 and another was shot there on 11 October 1861 (x, 43, 518).]

Larks

68 Skylark [Sky Lark *Alauda arvensis*]

Abundant. A specimen of a pale buff colour was kill'd at Falmouth.

[When this pale bird was shot is not recorded, but on 23 October 1816, a "perfectly white" lark was shot at Point, Feock (*WB*, 25 x). Albinos often attracted the attention of the press, such as the white Woodcock shot at Caerhays in December 1813 (*WB*, 24 xii).

On 8 June 1826, when Couch was "Riding in the Country at 26 minutes past 2 o'Clock in the morning two or three Larks rose from the ground in full song; cloudy weather and no moon" (iv, 139), and similarly at 2.10 a.m. on 14 June 1835 (vi, 159). The 1826 species is not specified, but Skylarks occasionally do sing at night, as does the Wood Lark. His early references tell of when the birds sing, which they do almost throughout the year, the appearance of winter flocks, as the first in 1813 on 23 November (i, 11), and asks in December 1815 why they "should continue here when their food is so scarce that thousands are starv'd, as in that severe winter while other Birds migrate" (i, 85-6).

A Lark "kept nearly six years in a Cage, & others for various periods, never wash, tho' water was often plac'd in the Cage; but when a turf in the Cage was sprinkl'd with water they rubb'd themselves on it; never doing so on the dry turf" (iv, 129-30, January 1835). This is hardly surprising for a species virtually confined to grassland.

In January 1850, Couch noticed a dearth of Sky Larks, perhaps due to the cold weather, but suggested that "the Custom of farmers to steep their Corn, previously to sowing it, in the solution of Sulphate of Copper, may have lessen'd their numbers, by poisoning them" (ix, 183). This admirable concern about conservation was perhaps unfounded; Bordeaux mixture (copper sulphate, quicklime and water) has long been an effective fungicide, but seldom "of major importance in damaging wild plants and animals" (K. Mellanby, 1967, *Pesticides and Pollution*, pp. 98-9).]

69 Woodlark [Wood Lark *Lullula arborea*]

Not abundant. It changes its quarters.

[Couch first recorded this species in 1817 (ii, 75): "The Woodlark must now be added to my list of Cornish Birds; for I have seen it sing as it flew, & descend & settle on a tree or bush. I have also heard a bird singing late at night which I suppose to be the same." For this reason the species has been mistaken for the Nightingale. The Wood Lark was always thinly distrubted in Cornwall and has declined since the 1960s with the last confirmed breeding in 1983. It remains an uncommon passage migrant and winter visitor.]

70 Rocklark [Rock Pipit *Anthus petrosus*]

Common on the Cliffs & beaches throughout Cornwall. Numbers of them are seen by fishermen, crossing the Channel from France, in Spring; generally in small flocks. This is the more extraordinary, as this Bird is common with us in the winter.

[British Rock Pipits are largely sedentary; what the fishermen saw were surely Meadow Pipits. There are comparatively few definite records of migrant Rock Pipits, generally Scandinavian birds, including the closely related Water Pipit (*A. spinoletta*) that is sparingly reported in Cornwall from October to March. Rock and Meadow Pipits, as well as larks, were confused in the early 19th century. Bewick also called the Rock Pipit a "Field Lark" (*Alauda campestris*), an inappropriate name that Couch used in 1824 when he called it "no stranger here" (iv, 42). Under the name Titlark, Couch noted Rock Pipits in 1816 (i, 99): "Feby. 6. Titlark begins to sing. The voice is low, & meagre, as if beginning to sing a lesson to which it has long been accustom'd. These Birds continue with us the whole year, wading up to the belly in the water after insects - every day in the year when the tide is out they may be found on the beach; but I never saw one in the garden. They will fly up into the air after insects, & then return, as I have before observ'd of the furze chatter" {Stonechat}.]

71 Titlark [Meadow Pipit *Anthus pratensis*]

Common. The Rocklark is call'd Titlark in Cornwall.

[Dialect Titlark usually applied to the Meadow Pipit, and it is not always clear which species Couch meant, as on 16 July 1816 when there were "Young Titlarks on the beach: the old ones have not frequented there since the commencement of the breeding Season" (ii, 26). Similarly, the "Shore Larks" seen by William Minards while tilling his potatoes near the cliff on 26 February 1856, "numerous shoals" of them "dropping in from the Sea through the day", were probably Meadow Pipits and not "Anthus Petrosus" that Couch meant (x, 290). Meadow Pipits breeding near the coast commonly forage along the tide-line during the rest of the year when they may out-number the Rock Pipits.]

72 Treelark [Tree Pipit *Anthus trivialis*]

In Summer.

[As a breeding species, the Tree Pipit has been mainly confined to the eastern half of the County, but has become increasingly rare since the 1960s. Couch makes no reference to it in his *Journals*.]

73 Grasshopper Lark [Common Grasshopper Warbler *Locustella naevia*]

Not uncommon, but shy.

[Couch should have been familiar with the grasshopper-like song of this warbler, but his only reference to the bird is in January 1820 when he examined and described in detail the mouth, tongue and windpipe of what he believed to be this species (iii, 51-52). If correct, it must have been obtained the previous summer, which seems unlikely unless the bird had been preserved by himself or Clement Jackson. Several were reported throughout the County in the summer of 1849 (*Pz*, 1849, p. 270) while in the second week of May 1851 Mr. G. Copeland shot one "on the Furze common, Pendennis", Falmouth (*TN*, 1851, p. 163). It is now an uncommon passage migrant, mainly in spring. It breeds mostly in moorland areas, notably on the Goss Moors and in some coastal localities.]

Wagtails
74 Pied Wagtail [*Motacilla alba*]

Common, & does not change its quarters.

[Couch means that his local birds were resident. In his *Journals*, Couch called this Ray's Wagtail or White Wagtail and was probably unaware that continental birds, the nominate race now known as the White Wagtail, augment our winter population. In 1815, he believed that birds in the north of England migrated south (i, 84), a notion he must have obtained from Ray (1678, p. 237), though this is only partially true, even for Scotland. In January 1816, he wrote: "I perceive a difference between two specimens of the White Wagtail - in one of them all the dark places are intensely black, which causes the white to appear very white; in the other the dark parts are greyish. I think this only a sexual difference" (i, 89-90). He was correct in part. The female tends to have a rather blotchy grey back, but he must also have seen the continental form that has noticeably paler, even grey upper parts, including the top of the head. Many British breeding birds do migrate in the autumn to the Atlantic coast of southern Europe, returning mainly in March and April. Thus, in April 1847, a local fisherman reported "that a short time since, & repeatedly, he has seen little parties of this Bird, 6 or 8 in number, flying hither across the Channel. They must separate immediately on arrival; for they are never seen {at Polperro} but singly or in pairs" (ix, 111). Autumn emigrants were seen "passing" in late August and early September 1848 (ix, 152).

Among his other early notes, Couch observed in February 1816 "that the white wagtail is master of the Redbreast, repeatedly driving it away from food", and later in the year "one follow'd a Swallow in several convolutions of its flight, in order to peck it; & I have observ'd one to persecute a Bird which I believe to be a Lark" (i, 100; ii, 57). Apart from seeing young on the beach at Polperro in June 1816 (ii, 19), Couch says nothing about any local breeding birds. "A Singular Occurrence" (*WB*, 8 ix 1848) he missed in the local paper was of a "Water Wagtail, commonly called Dish-washer, {that} built her nest and hatched her young in the cage of a whim, during its constant revolution both day and night" at Wheal Cherry, a mine in Lelant.]

75 Grey Wagtail [*Motacilla cinerea*]

I have never seen it in Summer; it usually comes in September, & goes away in March. I have never seen it with the black on the breast, which it lacks in winter. [Added later] A pair staid with us thro' the Summer 1834, & bred, & so since.

[In spite of heading his account with the currently accepted English name, Couch frequently called this species the Yellow Wagtail in his *Journal*, as do many people today. That he meant the Grey is proved by his use of the old scientific name *Motacilla boarula*. Why he should have called it Yellow is unclear because he frequently consulted Ray (1678) who named all three species of wagtails correctly.

The Grey was scarcer at Polperro than the Pied, noting in June 1816 that "it goes to more retir'd places to breed than the white wagtail does; & in consequence is little seen in summer by us" (ii, 22). The pair that nested in 1834 and later, did so at Crumplehorn (vi, 82). He referred to them at greater length in his *Illustrations of Instinct* (1847, p. 136): "... a single pair, which successfully built a nest, have left a colony of residents, who neither depart in summer, nor perceptibly increase in winter". Breeding birds may well have been scarce throughout the south-west because Edward Moore (1830, p. 305-6) also regarded it as a winter visitor to south Devon, but believed "that they occasionally do breed here; as I have seen a pair in June, in the neighbourhood of Buckland Abbey", while Rodd noted breeding "annually on the banks of the Lynher" (*RRIC*, 1840, p. 76).]

76 Yellow Wagtail [*Motacilla flava*]

Never in Summer, most common in Spring & Autumn.

[Couch crossed out "Spring", and in his published 1838 account wrote that it was rarer than the other wagtails, "and in Autumn and Winter only". Couch was confused. Yellow Wagtails are summer visitors. His winter sightings were surely wrongly identified Greys. There is nothing in his *Journal* to show that he ever saw a genuine Yellow Wagtail, a species that bred at Marazion Marsh until 1965. See also **233** in the Supplement.]

Warblers

77 Redbreast [European Robin *Erithacus rubecula*]

Common in our Gardens at all seasons. It moults early & resumes its song the first of our Autumnal Birds, chanting most & best in wet weather. Dates when it has resumed its song, August 12, 1816; 13th 1819; 17th 1828; 18th 1822, 1829; 21st 1824; Sepr. 1, 1824; 5th 1823.

[Robins cease singing mainly between mid-June and mid-July. There are few song birds to compete with it in autumn and winter. Indeed, winter breeding is well attested for this and other song birds in

Britain. Richard Abraham, the Miller, informed Couch that in the second week in January 1849 "a Robin's nest was found in a Garden with two eggs in it" (ix, 159). Such records attracted the local press: a Robin's nest with five eggs near Helston on Christmas Day 1843 was probably the same with four young "apparently doing well" in a bullock house near Helston the following month (*WB*, 5 & 26 i 1844). "As proof of the extreme mild season" in December 1818, a Robin's nest with five eggs in it" was found at the appropriately named Robin Tink's Quarry, Padstow, while in the same town was the nest of a "grey thrush" (Mistle or Song Thrush) "with young ones quite in a callow state" (*WB*, 18 xii). A Wren's nest with young birds "was this week found in the neighbourhood of Truro (*WB*, 20 xii 1811).

One of Couch's earliest observations, on 24 April 1810, was watching a Robin carrying a blade of grass to a nest, " a day or two after the young had left the eggs. I looked at it with a spyglass" (i, 3), the first evidence that he used a telescope to watch birds.

Not unexpectedly, Couch commented on the confiding nature of the Robin in August 1816: "birds in general consume the noxious & the waste of nature's store; but from their timidity many things escape them; in particular angles {worms} and small slugs, which are destructive in gardens, quickly bury them themselves, & would always escape, was not the redbreast endow'd with such confidence as to attend very close at the heels of the workman" (ii, 27-8).]

78 Redstart [Common Redstart *Phoenicurus phoenicurus*]
Exceedingly scarce, & I believe never seen in Summer. One was taken in an house at Falmouth Octr 26, 1822 [*J*, v, 74], & I believe I have seen one or two in winter.
[Couch confused the Common and the Black Redstart (*P. ochruros*), as did all naturalists. John Gould added the latter to the British list in 1829 after he had examined one taken at Kilburn, London, on 25 October. Migrants could be either species and would not always have been easy to separate; one seen by Stephen Clogg on Looe Island in the first week of April 1852 was assumed to be the Common (x, 66).

Only the Black Redstart is seen in winter in Cornwall. The following of Couch's records most probably refer to the Black: December 1822, "A Bird has been brought to my house, but not being present I did not see it; it is thus describ'd to me. About the size of a sparrow - body & head dark, nearly black - tail red" (iii, 152). 19 November 1824: "I have today seen a bird about the size of the redbreast, ash colour'd on the back & head, tail red - Is this the redstart? It flew up to take insects like the furze Chat, & after a little while flew westward" (iv, 71). Because only the back and head are described as ash coloured, this latter record could be a late migrant Common Redstart.

Couch was not aware that the Common Redstart bred in Cornwall until 1844 when E. H. Rodd informed him that it "has certainly had its nest & bred at Trebartha" in North Hill (viii, 340). It is strange that Couch had overlooked this because Rodd had already noted its breeding at Trebartha Hall by 1840 (*RRIC*, 1840, p. 76). R. J. Julian reported that one or two pairs bred at Mount Edgcumbe (*TN*, 1851, p. 86-87). If it can be believed, a pair reared five young in a pigeon hole in Liskeard in 1859. Four young were taken and put in a cage; the adults not only fed them but contrived their escape through the bars the following day (x, 444; *RCG*, 1 vii).]

79 Dartford Warbler [*Sylvia undata*]
Rather scarce, but not migrant. I have seen a pair shot near Looe in winter.
[Clement Jackson showed Couch on 20 January 1829 the pair shot at Hannafore, Looe. "Others were there; & he says he understands them to have bred there" (v, 61). The Dartford Warbler was first discovered in Cornwall by Col. George Montagu near The Tolmen Stone, Constantine, in September 1796. Nicholas Hare was given a nest in 1849 containing five eggs, "believed by all who have seen it to be that of a Dartford Warbler. The nest was found the last week in May, at the foot of a hedge, near St Cleer Common" (*Pz*, 1849, p.314-5).]

80 Blackstart [Black Redstart *Phoenicurus ochruros*]
[The name is written at the bottom of a page with no space for any comment, nor is it mentioned in his published 1838 account. Passage migrants and winter visitors are not uncommon, numbers varying annually. See also Common Redstart above and **232** in Supplement.]

81 Hedge Sparrow [Hedge Accentor or Dunnock *Prunella modularis*]
Common thro' the Year. Large Excrescences are often observ'd on the bill and the legs.
[The "excrescences" were observed by Clement Jackson (*MNH*, 1830, Vol.3, p.176) and must be one of the earliest published references to the condition popularly known as "grotty foot" by bird ringers. It is unlikely to be noticed unless the bird is handled. The phenomenon was overlooked in early ornithological works except by William Macgillivray (1839, *A History of British Birds*, Vol. 2, p. 256) who had "several times shot individuals thus affected" by "tubercular and apparently carcinomatous excrescences upon the eyelids and about the base of the bill". They are more common around the legs and caused by the mite *Knemidocoptes mutans* that feeds on ceratin under the scales of the legs. The Sedge Warbler is the only other species so afflicted.

The Dunnock was the first bird studied in detail by Couch, from the building of the nest on 13 March 1816 to quitting it on 16 April. On 7 April the nestlings "are much grown" and he describes the development of their feathers, the large eyes "cover'd by the integuments; tho' I believe I can see where the eyelids will be" and so forth (i, 103, 107, 110-2, 114).]

82 Wheatear [Northern Wheatear *Oenanthe oenanthe*]

Common on the grassy margin of Cliffs, arriving in small parties in succession, about the middle of March, at an early hour in the morning. None come across the Sea so late as noon. It is sometimes met with in Winter; when it changes colour entirely, except the rump, which always remains white. The rest of the body is light brown, the quill & tail feathers edg'd with brown; breast & belly paler. Our Boys call it Knacker.

Wheatear, after Ray

[The male Wheatear retains its grey back in non-breeding plumage. Records of true wintering birds are exceptional, but migrants may remain late in the year. At first, Couch had difficulty in identifying this bird "which is very common with us all the Summer ... on the edge of the cliffs", but rightly concluded in December 1815 that it had to be the Wheater (i, 80-81). The following March, from his careful examination of some birds, he was able to show that the illustration in "Newberry's Natural History" is "very exact", while that in the 2nd edition of Gregory's Cyclopaedia "is not correct" (i, 104-5). Gregory's is George Gregory's *Dictionary*, 2nd ed. 1813. Newberry (*sic*) has to be J. Newbery who published in 1763 *The Natural History of Birds*, the second volume of Dr Richard Brookes' *A System of Natural History*. His description of the Wheatear, without an illustration, is a résumé of Ray (1678) in which it is illustrated.

Couch mostly noted arrival or departure dates, as on 5 April 1816 when he saw two in The Warren, Polperro, and "in about half an hour, many ... that arriv'd from the west, by land, & not from the Seaward" (i, 109-10). In 1864, birds arrived early, his first on 7 March (xi, 85). Most pairs breed in Cornwall on Bodmin Moor and records from the south coast are now rare. On 11 June 1816, Couch noted "Wheatear has eggs", and on the 21st, "Young Wheatears flying about" (ii, 19 & 21).

"Knacker" may, like the more widespread "Chack" and similar names, relate to its call note. The usual Cornish dialect was "White Ass".]

83 Stone Chat [Stonechat *Saxicola torquata*]

Common.

[The Stonechat is a well distributed resident of the wilder parts of the Cornish coast, so it is not surprising that Couch commented on the bird's habits. He was particularly struck in 1815 by its "consequential" or pompous attitude when perched on the top of a furze bush, thinking it "ridiculous" when "contrasted with the size of the bird" (i, 82). In May 1816, he found its song to be "agreeable", previously having "consider'd this Bird as furnish'd with no other note than its common harsh chatter" (ii, 1).

It was William Minards who furnished Couch in 1835 with information on the Stonechat's nest: "two or three times in his lifetime he has found the nest of this common Bird; but the reason of its rarity proceeds from its being so very cunningly concealed. It builds either on the ground, or in very tarn (that is short) furze; but even if the nest is on one side, the entrance is at a great distance, & on the opposite side; this entrance being perhaps a couple of yards from the nest, & along a cover'd passage. He thinks also that in case of need, the old Bird escapes by another opening" (vii, 32).

British birds tend to move closer to the coast in winter, but some British and many continental birds are migratory, though the following record is late for a spring passage. In June 1837, "A furze chat alighted on a Boat at about 6 leagues from land - coming from Seaward - it flew at last towards land" (vii, 221).]

84 Reed Warbler [Sedge Warbler *Acrocephalus schoenobaenus*]
Rare. Its Song has been mistaken for that of the Nightingale, a Bird that I feel certain, has never been found in Cornwall. [Added later] In some Seasons it seems to abound.
[Couch used the old scientific name *Motacilla salicaria* for the Sedge Warbler, a species first distinguished by Thomas Pennant and Gilbert White between 1766 and 1769. It was White who noted its habit of singing at night and, hence, its confusion with the Nightingale. In July 1821, a bird "heard singing late at night in the valley above Palace Shute", on the east side of Polperro, attracted local attention because it was assumed to be a Nightingale. Couch watched the nesting bird with his telescope, his description of this "Reed Sparrow" fitting that of the Sedge Warbler (iii, 117-8). Couch saw young in the willows in his garden, "attended by their Parents" on 27 July 1821 (iii, 119).

The true Reed Warbler (*A. arundinaceus*) was certainly a very rare summer migrant throughout the 19th century with no confirmation of breeding in Cornwall until 1945 on the lower reaches of the Tamar. Couch's only reference to an undoubted Reed Warbler (ix, 179) was for 1849 when several were captured in the autumn on Scilly, "not known as Cornish until then" (Rodd, *Pz*, 1850, p. 407).]

85 White Throat [Common Whitethroat *Sylvia communis*]
Common in Summer.
[Couch first described the species seen when walking near Talland in May 1816 and the discovery of a nest containing two young and two addled eggs, built in the stock of a pollarded sycamore tree, the following month (ii, 7, 20). He became familiar with its song the following May (ii, 84), but made few other notes on the bird. In 1845, he wrote that they usually built a nest in his "plantation", but not that year, with no bird seen until the end of July. The previous year they had nested undisturbed (ix, 24-25). The Whitethroat is more numerous near the Cornish coast than well inland.]

86 Wood Wren [Wood Warbler *Phylloscopus sibilatrix*]
Common in woods near Looe & Leskeard [Liskeard].
[Couch transposed the old scientific name *Sylvia trochilus* (Willow Warbler) for this species with *S. sylvicola* (Wood Warbler), but his very brief comments reveal his error. Nicholas Hare was given an egg from a clutch of five taken from a nest in the Liskeard area in May 1849 (*Pz*, 1849, p. 315). The Wood Warbler has always been a scarce species in Cornwall, mainly confined to wooded valleys south and east of Bodmin Moor. Couch makes no mention of it in his *Journals*, the Polperro area being an unsuitable habitat for breeding birds.]

87 Willow Wren [Willow Warbler *Phylloscopus trochilus*]
Common.
[William Minards, out fishing in May 1816, reported four birds he called "Miller's Thum(b)s" which alighted on his boat in misty weather. They were brought ashore exhausted and released. Couch took these to be Willow Wrens, though he did not see them (ii, 14-15). At the end of May he wrote (ii, 19), "The Birds I have call'd Willow Wrens are not seen now with us; I conclude therefore that they only visit us in passing to their old haunts". Miller's Thumb was a name applied to the Willow Warbler, Wood Warbler, Chiffchaff and even the Goldcrest in various parts of the country, so is of no help in determining what William Minards really saw.

Nevertheless, Willow Warblers should have been common enough in the Polperro area. In May 1829, Couch found them "in very great plenty this Summer in thick hedges of willow, in retir'd places close to a stream of water" (v, 71-72). He supposed it was this species that arrived about 12 April 1816 (i, 118), yet curiously he never mentioned this warbler's distinctive and beautiful song.]

Willow Warbler (left), Wood Warbler (centre) and Chiffchaff, after Bewick

88 Lesser Petty Chaps [Common Chiffchaff *Phylloscopus collybita*]
Sometimes abundant in retir'd bushy places about running streams, having much the manner of the Wren, but more shy. My friend Mr Jackson shot a specimen in January 1829, near Looe.
[In the same passage that Couch described the abundance of the "Willow Wren" in May 1829, he also wrote that the "Lesser Willow Wren" was equally common, describing its action as that of "a Wren {i.e. warbler}, & flies like it. It keeps in the thicket of the hedge, is restless, & will not fly out of the hedge, if a person be near it, so that it is not easily examin'd at liberty". The above description of the Lesser Pettychaps is evidently based on this 1829 account (v, 71-72). "Lesser" is an error for "Least" Willow Wren, used by Bewick.

Clement Jackson's specimen in January 1829 was the first found wintering in Cornwall, a habit now common and widespread in the County. Col. George Montagu was the first to discover it wintering in Britain in south Devon in 1806-1807.]

89 Golden Crown'd Wren [Goldcrest *Regulus regulus*]
Common, about woods.

[Clement Jackson was the informant of Couch's interesting account of migrants in November 1844: "on the 2nd & 3rd of Novr. there were hundreds of these Birds on Looe Island (where there is no shelter except a few low furze bushes) - they continued 3 or 4 days, but their coming & going were not notic'd. The wind was hard at S & SE which probably drove them thither in their migration across the Channel. They were exceedingly tame, & some of them took food from the hands of the Coast Guard Men there. They ate flies: but a Blow fly was too large for one of them to deal with, & the men were oblig'd to tear it in pieces before it could be swallow'd" (ix, 6). Such migrations were already well known in Britain, but this is the first recorded for Cornwall. Couch also noted them "in numbers ... thro' the winter months" in January 1849 (ix, 159).]

90 Wren [Winter Wren *Troglodytes troglodytes*]
Common. One with a white ring round its neck.

[Early *Journal* records note nest-building and the departure of young, but particularly the dates of singing, finding in 1817 that song occurred throughout most of the year (ii, 67). Couch was well aware that Wrens build several nests in a season and that only one is used, but in 1834 William Minards told him of an unfinshed, unused nest in which he found one evening "four full grown young ... which must have taken shelter there for the evening, perhaps led by their parents" (vi, 85).

William was also responsible for a more interesting account given to Couch in October 1835: "on his own knowledge, that in a severe winter, these Birds have been accustomed to cluster for warmth. In one case in a hole in an hedge, where the moss abounded, he found a Cluster or ball, as large as a globular quarts measure: & in a short distance in the hedge were three or four of these clusters, all together little less than an hundred. This clustering is not uncommon; & when Wrens are seen thus to act, or to creep into holes of trees, it tokens a cold night. A Wren prefers the haystack before the Corn Mow" (vii, 35). This is the largest gathering of its kind recorded from Cornwall. Couch also noted (ix, 106) from the *West Briton*, 8 i 1847, that Roger Braddon of Treglith, Treneglos, had discovered one evening the week before, 55 in a hole in the thatch of a barn. The British record for Wrens in a nest-box is 60 in February 1969 in Norfolk, the birds taking twenty minutes to emerge.]

Flycatchers

91 Spotted Flycatcher [*Muscicapa striata*]

Common in Summer.

[Couch makes no mention of this widespread species in his *Journal*. It's numbers have declined in recent years.

The Pied Flycatcher *Ficedula hypoleuca* was not reported in Cornwall until one was shot in March 1838 at Mount Edgcumbe, Maker (J. C. Bellamy, 1839, p. 204). Couch noted its occurrence in autumn 1849 (ix, 179, 224) when one was obtained from Alverton, Penzance, and another on Scilly about the beginning of October (*Pz*, 1849, p. 271; 1850, p. 405).]

92 Creeper [Eurasian Treecreeper *Certhia familiaris*]

Common in Gardens in Autumn, for a few days, & then passing on. Common in Spring in retir'd orchards.

[This has always been a thinly distributed woodland and parkland resident in Cornwall. Couch first noted it on 1 August 1816: "I have seen a Bird in our orchard, which I take to be the common oxeye, or as it is call'd Certhia familiaris, but which is not common with us" (ii, 28). The song of the Treecreeper is rather thin and high-pitched; what Couch first considered to be its song he discovered in May 1817 was that of the Whitethroat, but his garden sighting need not be doubted (ii, 83-84).

Dialect "Oxeye" usually referred to the Great Tit and Oxeye Creeper for the present species, an outmoded name even in Couch's day.]

Titmice

93 Greater Titmouse [Great Tit *Parus major*]

Commonest of the Genus.

[The Blue Tit has generally been accepted as the commonest of the tits since Walter Moyle of Bake, St Germans, described it as such in 1720. Couch was not familiar with all the tits in 1816 when he was told on 11 June that at Trelawne, Pelynt, "three species frequent the garden" (ii, 19). He knew the "Greater" and a "smaller not noticed in Gregory's Cyclopedia" (George Gregory, 1806, 2nd ed. 1813). In 1815, Couch said the Great Tit "frequents our gardens during the autumn & winter" (i, 55), though it was surely resident then, and on 29 June 1826 he heard one calling "several times at 1 o'Clock at night" (iv, 141).]

94 Blue Titmouse [Blue Tit *Parus caeruleus*]

[Couch makes no comment. In 1838 he describes it as "Common, but more wandering in its habits than the Great Titmouse". His earliest references to "Titmice" probably mean this species, but are equally applicable to the others. He was much impressed with the method of searching for insects, as on 19 May 1816 in his apple tree: "not a tuft of blossom seem'd to escape it", yet it does not "seem to injure the blossom, tho' once or twice a petal was observed to drop; & the celerity with which it proceeds, seem'd to be without care. But the little injury this Bird can do, must be compensated by the good that is effected by the destruction of Insects, which at this time are so plentiful among the tufts of blossom" (ii, 8).]

95 Cole Titmouse [Coal Tit *Parus ater*]

[Couch makes no comment and it seems the species cannot have been well known around Polperro. On 28 February 1829 (v, 63) he records seeing one and a Marsh Tit at Clement Jackson's, both having been shot in Cornwall. In his 1838 account, Couch described the Coat Tit as "local". It may well have been scarce throughout much of the 19th century and only increased as a consequence of afforestation. James Clark (1906) noted a greater population in firs and plantations in the east of the County.]

96 Longtailed Tit [Long-tailed Tit *Aegithalos caudatus*]

Common, in retir'd places, in small Companies, which seem to be one family.

[Family parties average about ten birds. They keep together throughout the winter in territories that they defend against other foraging groups. The only *Journal* record is for early 1830 when Couch saw them in cold weather (v, 110).]

97 Marsh Titmouse [Marsh Tit *Parus palustris*]

Scarce.

[Marsh Tits frequent both moist and dry habitats with some preference for the former. (See also under Coal Tit above.) The very similar Willow Tit *P. montanus* was not recognised as a British species until 1900; scattered colonies breed in the upper Fowey valley, on Goss Moor and similar localities.]

98 Bearded Titmouse [Bearded Tit *Panurus biarmicus*]

[Couch makes no entry; hardly surprising when no record was published until 1846 when a male was shot in a "sedgy bottom" near St Levan church about 28 January. J. T. Blight illustrated it in his *A Week at the Land's End* (1861, p. 142) when the bird was in E. H. Rodd's collection. An earlier

Bearded Tit, after Blight

specimen had been obtained near Bosahan, St Anthony-in-Meneage, and was in the collection of Humphry Millett Grylls of Bosahan (died 17 April 1834) until it passed into the hands of I. P. Magor of Redruth (*Z*, 1846, p.1298). The latter may have been the one seen on 8 October 1845 by W. P. Cocks "in Cornwall" (ix, 56).]

Swallows
99 Swallow [Barn Swallow *Hirundo rustica*]

Common.

First Swallow Seen. April 4th, 1821; 10th, 1808; 11th, 1834; 13th, 1827; 15th, 1830; 16th, 1818, 1824, 1833; 17th, 1828, 1832, 1836; 21st, 1811, 1821, 1822; 26th, 1825; 28th, 1823; 30th, 1820; May 2, 1812, 1815. [1863, 5 May (*J*, xi 52);1864, 29 Mar, at Par (*J*, xi, 94); 1866, 20 Apr. (*J*, xi, 195)]

Disappearance. Sepr. 24, 1816; 28th, 1820; 30th, 1818, 1833; Octr. 2, 1823, 1831, 1832; 3rd, 1825, 1830, 1836; 7th, 1824; 11th, 1815, 1834; 29th, 1819; Nov. 1, 1805; 16th, 1834.

(Some of these dates were added later, as were some for the migratory species that follow.)

[Couch's first two entries in his *Journal* are to Swallows and House Martins; both flying about Polperro until 1 November 1805, and Swallows arriving on 10 April 1806 (i, 1). He was particularly interested in migration and published a note as early as 1822 (*IM*). More appeared in his account dated 22 June 1831, "Notes on the Chimney Swallow and on the Window Swallow or Marten" (*MNH*, iv, pp. 520-523). Here it become clear that the earliest date on which Couch saw "either species" for himself was 19th April (year not given). The Swallow on 4 April 1831 (v, 151) had been seen by a fisherman near the Eddystone, while "again, a company of four was seen on the 13th {1827} at sea, flying low, and making towards land, at 3 o'clock p.m." Thomas Holten also told him that on 11 May 1832 he saw "hundreds or more ... at about twelve leagues from land flying towards our Coast, about mid day" (vii, 284). The earliest spring record was on 23 March 1849: Tom Curtis "while at sea - saw two Swallows fly over his Boats, & one of them fell dead on the water close to him". Couch added a quote (*RCG*, 23 iii 1849) that two were sighted on Sunday 18th at Roscraddock, St Cleer, the seat of the Rev. G. P. Norris (ix, 161).

Swallows and House Martins left early in the dry, hot summer of 1865: "I do not think I have seen one since the middle of September, & they may have gone away even before that date" (xi, 165). Of autumn migrants, Couch noted that on 7 October 1835, "in the evening, just at the time when Drift Boats go out to fish (& consequently about an hour before Sunset) an intelligent fisherman of Looe inform'd Mr Jackson that he saw a large flock of Swallows fly away to the southward, over the Sea: - there can be no doubt that this was a migration" (vii, 48). Close observation in 1816 showed him how the Swallows' forked tails were "admirably adapted for their circuits in the air, for by furling or depressing one half they are able to act on the air with the other half, like the rudder of a ship" (i, 101).

In the autumn of 1831, Swallows were seen flying in and out of a cave to the west of Polperro known locally as Swallow's Hole. Nesting was suspected here and confirmed the following year (vi, 19, 25). "The Cave is on the west side of the Great Cove; is not remarkably high, but except at low water is not accessible, but by Boats; it is not dark, & not, I should think, above thirty feet high; in its roof is an opening, the extremity of which I could not clearly discern; but into which the Swallows flew & rested for some time; then flew on again. There can therefore, I think, be no doubt but that their nests are in this place". In his *Illustrations of Instinct* (1847), he added "that although the cavern is openly exposed to the observations of persons continually passing it, the birds shew no hesitation in flying in, however numerous the observers, yet the precise spot where the nest is so well concealed as to be not easily found; and the birds will not enter it if an observer takes his station within the secluded space so as to be in view of it". Cave nests were uncommon in Couch's day and have not been reliably reported in Cornwall since the early 1900s, though cave nests of House Martins are still widespread. When Couch told Clement Jackson about the cave-nesting Swallows at Polperro, Jackson replied "that near Falmouth he knew a Cavern where numbers of Martins built; the side of the Roof was studded with their Nests. What renders the fact more remarkable is that whilst the Martins built in the inner part, a pair of Kestrels had their nest just under a projecting ledge at the entrance" (vi, 1832, 20). The site of Couch's Swallow's Hole is marked on the 6 inch O.S. map (1908 edition) as Swallow Cove (SX 2045 5055).

The Barn Swallow was formerly commonly known as the Chimney Swallow, and in 1832, "In Mrs Billing's kitchen chimney, on the outside, not far from the top, are two cavities, resembling Pigeon holes. In one of these, this year, a Pair of Swallows have built their Nest" (vi, 25).]

100 Martin [House Martin *Delichon urbica*]

Common.

Martin arriv'd. Apl. 20, 1816, 1835; 21st, 1829; 22nd, 1819; 23rd, 1818; 24th, 1810, 1821; 30th, 1823. May 2, Martins 1812, 1815, 1820; 3rd, 1817; 5th, 1825.

Disappearance, Septr. 28, 1820; 31st, 1818. Octr. 2, 1823; 3rd, 1825; 4th, 1836; 5th, 1819; 11th, 1815, 1816, 1821, 1828, 1829; 13th, 1817; 14th, 1822; 15th, 1824, 1827; 25th, 1834; 27th, 1813. Novr. 1, 1805; 6th, 1810; [21st, 1864 (*J*, xi, 122); 28th, 1844 (*J*, ix, 7)]. Decr. 7, 1835.

[The following account is the one published in modified form in *MNH*, iv, 1831, noted above under Swallow. Couch wrote his MS notes with only two paragraphs; I have added more for easier reading.]

Very few migratory Birds have attracted so much observation as those of the Swallow tribe, chiefly on account of the regularity of their movements, & their taking up of their abode so near to the residence of Man. But tho' thus offering themselves continually to his observation, a satisfactory account of their migrations, & especially of the motives to it, can scarcely be said to be obtained as yet; nor is it likely to be the case until observations have been made for a longer period, & in different quarters of the world. It is with this in view that I record the notes of the arrival & departure of the Swallows & Martin, together with the following incidental observations.

These Birds reach the land near the shore, & in misty weather seem to have difficulty in making it; for I have been assur'd by intelligent fishermen that when the weather is hazy Swallows, Martins, Swifts, Wheatears & a bird which they denominate a Miller's Thumb, & which is, I believe the Reed Wren [the name was given to various warblers of the Chiffchaff type] will alight on their boats when three or four leagues from land, either singly or in small flocks; and they appear so much fatigued that even the strong wing'd Swallow is only able to fly from one end of the boat to another when they attempt to seize it [Story from William Curtis, May 1816 (*J*, ii, 13)]. Wheatears are often so worn out, as to drop dead in the boat. The Swallow & Martin come in small parties, & if they do not happen to be our own residents, soon pass onto their accustom'd haunts; so that after two or three have been seen, it may perhaps be a fortnight before others make their appearance.

The extraordinary Confidence which these Birds repose in Man, in placing their nests in the midst of his dwellings, whilst most other Birds seek the most secret places, is worthy of notice; & serves to explain a circumstance which is singular in the feather'd race: I allude to the fact of their singing when in their Nests; which can only take place where there is no desire of concealment. The nest of the Swallow is commonly placed in a chimney thro' which no smoke passes; but I have known it built on the rafters within a deserted house; & at Trelawny house a Swallow has for several years found an entrance thro' a loophole in a Turret, & fix'd its nest against a door.

The Martin builds its nest of similar materials under the eaves of houses, & usually dedicates a few hours in the morning to the work, leaving it to dry during the remainder of the day. However, I have known them neglect a fine morning, & carry on the work thro' the Afternoon [May 1816 (*J*, ii, 5)], from no other apparent reason than the facility of procuring mud at that period, from a small distance, in a place which in the morning was cover'd by the tide. In selecting a place for the Nest, they are much influenced by its affording them a favourable fall in taking flight; & I have known them forsake a situation in which they had been accustomed to build beyond the memory of Man, only because a low wall had been erected, that in some measure interfer'd with their flight.

Towards the end of the Season these Birds congregate in rather large Companies, on the roof of an house, about a Tower, or other favourable situation, from which some are continually taking flight, & to which others are perpetually returning. This congregation seems to arise only from a sociable disposition; yet it continues, for perhaps six weeks, until the party becomes reduc'd, by the migration of small parties, to a very small number; which at last follow their companions, & are seen no more. My experience corroborates the remark that the Swallow tribe disappear earliest in the warmest Seasons. This seems to be a mysterious circumstance but may be explain'd by reference to the Constitution of the birds. It is well known that a certain temperature is necessary for hatching the eggs of birds; & that if this be exceeded the death of the young ones is the result. Instructed by this, the domestic fowl quits her nest for a considerable time in warm weather, that the eggs may be properly cool'd. The temperature adapted to the incubation of most tropical birds, is too great for the Eggs of the Cuckow & Swallow; under the direction therefore of a guiding providence which has implanted those feelings within them, they pass to more northern Regions, in search of a temperature congenial to their impressions.

When this great Object has been accomplish'd the body becomes prepared for another service. The Birds which remain in this Country thro' the Year, require the warm temperature of Autumn to enable them to moult. A certain degree of feverish action is necessary to this process; & by raising it artificially & prematurely, Bird catchers are known to accelerate the process of moulting. This fever, as the disorder of the same name in the human body, is accompanied with a morbid sensibility, that renders highly painful those impressions of the air, which before were pleasing. Instigated by these new sensations they take flight towards warmer regions; & having there accomplish'd the natural process of renewing the plumage again they seek a cooler air.

In many instances the Martin has been known to remain late, for the purpose of feeding its young, which from accidental Causes have not been brought to early maturity; & the moulting fever does not approach until the breeding constitution is ended, this does not commonly produce inconvenience. But sometimes the approach of the fever is felt before the young are able to fly; in which Case parental fondness gives way to febrile excitment, & I have known them left to perish in the Nest. It is remarkable that in the few instances in which summer Birds have been found torpid in conceal'd places, mention is made of their being discover'd naked: a circumstance that shews both the necessity of the moulting process, & the importance of a warm temperature to the expulsion of the new plumage. These observations further give us to see how a warm Summer by inducing the moulting fever early, causes their early departure; a cold season delays them by retarding it.

At the time of departure the numbers of our resident Birds lessen gradually; & those that go away together soon separate on the journey, only a very few remaining in one Company. Neither do they proceed in haste; for those which I have seen migrating, seem to be employ'd in hawking for prey as usual. We may suppose however, that when they have to cross the Ocean, they employ their utmost speed, in order to reach the opposite shore. The following notes will confirm the remark that these birds pass off in small Companies, & that those from more northern Regions are often seen in the passage after our own Birds have departed.

In 1819 Swallows were gone from our neighbourhood by the 29th of Septr & Martins on the 5th of October; yet on the 29th of Octr, two Swallow appeared, during a snow shower. They settled wherever they could find a place, not standing, but lying on the belly, as if the feet were benumb'd. They were persecuted by sparrows, &

annoy'd by the gaze of spectators; and finally pass'd onwards to the westward.

1825. Two hirundines, I believe Martins, flying about in the afternoon ten days after all our Birds had departed; the same happen'd two days after.

1827. Our Martins departed Octr 14. On the 29th of November Two Martins arriv'd in the afternoon & continued hawking for flies. The week previous there had been frost & snow, with the therm. 44° at noon; last night was a storm, today the therm. 51°; probably therefore these birds were blown out of their Course.

In 1828 our Martins departed Octr 11th; but on the 9th of November a few appear'd at Looe. No one can suppose that these were the same Birds which had remain'd with us during the Summer; & that, tho' diligently watch'd, they had escap'd observation for a month.

[Couch's long explanation for the reasons governing migration dates would not be accepted now. The simple fact is that in good summers food is readily available to feed the young. Departure of breeding birds may well be delayed in cool, wet summers when insects in particular are harder to find. Birds will abandon late broods when insufficient can be found both to feed young and build up their own fat reserves necessary for a long migration. The main stimulus to migration is the bird's "internal clock" controlled by the pituitary gland, but external factors are very important. H. N. Southern showed in the late 1930s that, in general, the Swallow's spring migration follows fairly closely the northward progress of the 48° F (9° C) isotherm, and the reverse can be inferred for the autumn (see *The Handbook of British Birds*, 1948 Ed., Vol. II, map p. 229).

House Martins are amongst the first birds Couch observed, including fatigued migrants that landed on the roofs on 27 October 1813, "where they remained with their eyes closed". He watched them on the window ledge of his house and "even opened the swing window without alarming them. After a time they flew about, as if in pursuit of prey. They continued with us two days, the wind being N & E, & cold, flying about; but in the evening of the third day, the wind got round to the West, & next morning not one was to be seen" (i, 12-3).

In May 1816, Couch was intrigued by a bird's efforts to span the gap between two foundation fragments of a nest with a piece of grass or straw. The grass was too long, so that when the ends were cemented in, the middle part sprung up too high "in a bent position ... when the bill was taken away", until at last "it was given up as a bad bargain". But by the following morning "the difficulty was remov'd, one end of the piece having been unloosed so that it lay smooth; whilst the end was jutting out from the mud wall of the nest" (ii, 12-3).

A nest was knocked down by a boy in 1858 at the lower mill in Polperro. The miller replaced it with a small round basket under the eaves, placing a board over most of the top. A pair reared three young in it, while a second pair built a nest "where the handle of the basket touched the overhanging eavestones" above the board and also reared young, though when Couch went to see it in August, the basket had been removed (x, 408-9).

1867. "Martins - a pair of these birds came to Mr Minard's house, where there were other nests, on the first days of the last week of July; and immediately they began a nest. But long before the nest was finished the female began to lay her eggs; & then it was that six other birds, I suppose her neighbours, set to work with their joint labours; and finished the nest for the new come pair. Their coming may have been caused by their being expelled from some other place" (xii, 59). On 18 August the same year, Couch observed something he had never seen before: "a pair enter & have their dwelling through a hole between the wall & the roof at our house on the Cliff. Close to this opening, into and out of which they seperately pass, is a clay built nest in the usual form, except that the hole of the entrance is at the side, not in front: the reason of which clearly is that the best fall for flight is in that direction; in consequence of the Coast Guard wall that is in front (xii, 62). In June 1868, a similar event occurred: "A nest, among several, having young ones in it; the opening was in one side - over which was a defect in the stone that caused a dripping that annoyed, or hurt, what was within. The Parents built up this opening with the usual materials and made an opening on the more sheltered side" (xii, 114).

Martin's nested at William Minard's house in Polperro for many years. In 1868 there were eight nests "and at the beginning of the Season one of them (and only one) was injured. The first pair that came took possession of this injured nest, and set about repairing it, although there appeared nothing to hinder them from taking possession of any one of the others, an apparent proof that this one had been their own in the last Season; & that they exercised local attachment to it. These 8 nests were occupied by 8 pairs; and of these of the first brood six nests produced four young ones in each: the other two nests produced three in each. All these nests had a second brood; of which two have three young ones in each, two have two young ones in each; and in the remaining four there are young which at this date {30 September} have not produced the young so as to be counted. The young of the 1st brood resorted to the nests of their parents - not only after the next eggs were laid - but occasionally sat on them - afterwards they clustered about the Nests by day - but when the new young were there they went elsewhere by night; not known where" (xii, 132). See also under Swallow above.]

101 Bank Martin [Sand Martin *Riparia riparia*]
Scarce, & in a few situations.

[No breeding colony has been recorded on the coast of south-east Cornwall. Couch's only reference to the species is for 12 April 1849 (ix, 164): "A Bank Martin is reported to me as arrived - of course a passenger" (i.e. a passage migrant). Mount's Bay has long contained breeding colonies, although the earliest noted by E. H. Rodd in J. S. Courtney (1845) have long been extinct: "common in the banks between Penzance and Marazion, and also on the road to Newlyn". The *Royal Cornwall Gazette* (17 v 1839) gave the arrival date of the "Bank Swallow" at Newlyn Green as 5 April 1839.]

102 Swift [Common Swift *Apus apus*]

Common.

Arrival. [3 Apr., at Looe, 1845, 28th, 1869]; May 1, 1824; 2nd, 1820, 1823; 3rd, 1827, 1828, 1829; 4th, 1830; 5th, 1819, 1825; 8th, 1817; 9th, 1826; 12th, 1831, 1835; 14th, 1822; 16th, 1821; 18th, 1818; 21st, 1816.

Departure. July 29, 1831; 31st, 1835. Aug. 2, 1818, 1819; 3rd, 1825; 9th, 1816, 1821, 1822; 11th, 1830; 13th, 1824; [16th, 1848]; 17th, 1823; [18th, 1849; 21st, 1836; 26th, 1837].

It is not long that Swifts have frequented my immediate neighbourhood. At first there were about two pairs; but have now increased to four or five Couples; but it is singular that according to my observations there is always an odd one. In migrating they depart all together; nor have I ever notic'd any one in its passage after our own Birds are gone. My friend Mr C. Jackson of Looe, who has had much experience in the setting up of Birds for preservation, & does it well, informs me that land Birds of cold climates have more fat & thinner skins than those of warm regions; & that the Swift has thicker skin than any other of our Birds according to its size.

[The reference to the thickness of fat and skin was an observation by Clement Jackson in 1828 (v, 31-2).

Couch soon realized that Swifts departed late in cool, wet summers, as in 1823 when "they did not go all at once, since there are four couples that frequent Polperro, of which I saw only one Couple for a few days previous to their final disappearance" (iii, 164-5). In contrast, in "the very great heat of the weather" in 1831, none was seen after 29 July (v, 156).

In the autumn of 1838, Couch used a ladder to examine the nesting site of Swifts in John Libby's house in Polperro, "near the new Association Meeting House". Two nests were excavated in soft mortar between the stones, one smaller than the other, and described them in great detail. The smaller, only six inches deep could not have contained more than one bird, while the larger, "a foot or more in depth, wider, but rather crooked" also contained an egg. He concluded that the male roosted in the smaller hole, leaving the larger for the female and young (viii, 11-13). His lengthy description was published in the *Naturalists' Note Book* in 1869. This is unusual, if correct, as both birds stay in the same nest. He makes no reference to Swifts nesting in cliff fissures, a habit probably now extinct in

Cornwall, though recorded at Camborne North Cliffs and elsewhere in the 1940s and suspected more recently.

Swifts do not normally land except at nest sites. They frequently roost at high altitude, though birds are known to rest on trees. William Minards saw one do just that on a thin upright branch of an Elm tree at Crumplehorn on 23 July 1841 (viii, 179). Couch kept a Swift in a cage in 1832 and noted its impressive grip, so firm that "allowing for the size of the Bird {it is} superior to that of the Buzzard", and "not until it began to grow weak" did it rest on the ground (vi, 23-24).]

103 Night Jar [European Nightjar *Caprimulgus europaeus*]
Common in Summer evenings in woods. It holds the same relation to the Swallow as the Owl to the Hawk. Its periods of migration are not well known. I have known one shot Novr 27, 1821; & they had ariv'd April 28, 1830 [*J*, v, 122].

Couch's watercolour of a Goatsucker or Nightjar

[Couch's watercolour drawing of the "Goatsucker" is probably the bird shot in 1821 for which he gave a full description (iii, 128). His reference to other birds is to show that the Nightjar is nocturnal like an owl, but insectivorous like the Swallow.

Clement Jackson heard the curious clapping noise made by its wings in flight in 1830 (v, 118), and killed one in 1832, "seen in broad Daylight pitch'd against the sloping branch of a tree" (vi, 20). On 18 September that year, Couch saw one "about our hills. I suspect in the act of migration" (vi, 72). On 27 April 1838, Jackson informed him that the summer migrants had arrived (vii, 283). One was shot at noon on 27 October 1848, "rous'd up from among the turnips" (ix, 152). The species is now a rare breeding bird in Cornwall.]

104 [Added later] White Bellied Swift [Alpine Swift *Apus melba*]
For the probability that this Bird has been seen in Cornwall, see my Journal Vol.7.
["John Minards informs me that he saw, last Summer {1835}, a large Swift with a cream coloured belly. It repeatedly flew past him, above Fishen-a-Bridge, and he might easily have shot it if he had had a gun. This can be no other than the Alpine Swift; and John is too accurate an Observer to be mistaken" (vii, 52). Fishing Bridge is where the road crosses the stream a quarter of a mile below Crumplehorn.

1842 (viii, 271; 1844, *Supplement*). "Mr Jackson sends me word that he has received an Alpine Swift - lately taken near the Land's End. He informs me, viva voce, that it flew on board a vessel, at 40 miles West of the Lands End, and was so fatigued as to be easily taken. This was about the middle of June." The *West Briton* of 12 August reported one "last week" in Clement Jackson's collection, but it may be the same bird, as must be Rodd's belief that Jackson had preserved one "taken near the Lizard" (*Pz*, 1850, p. 415). One in Rodd's collection had been shot by R. A. Daniel at Mylor on 24 October 1859 (*RCPS*, 1860, p. 95).

In his 1838 account, Couch referred to two having been seen in Cornwall without giving any details. The first must refer to the 1835 sighting, but the second remains a mystery. The Index to *Journal* vii gives pages 52 (the 1835 bird) and 86 (1836), but none is mentioned on p. 86 or near it.]

Pidgeons

105 Ringdove [Common Wood Pigeon *Columba palumbus*]
Common. [See also **106** and **108**.]

106 Rock Pidgeon [Rock Pigeon *Columba livia*]
[Couch makes no comment other than to note that T. C. Eyton (1836, p. 27) "shows that these references are to the Wood Pidgeon". However, what Eyton figures as a Wood Pigeon is the Stock Dove (now

Rock Pigeon, wrongly called a Stock Dove, after Bewick

officially called Stock Pigeon *Columba oenas*). Bewick (1826, p. 309) illustrated a Rock Pigeon for his "Wild Pigeon" (Stock Dove, *C. oenas*) and noted that there were "small differences" between the Stock Dove, Rock Pigeon and Wood Pigeon, but that they "may be included under the same denomination". It only emphasises the confusion that existed in the early 19th century over the species' differentiation. In his 1838 account, Couch calls the Rock Pigeon "Common in rocky Caverns on the Coast, but scarcely abundant". In December 1836, he saw them about Christmas, noting that "It had been hinted to me that this Bird goes from us in winter" (vii, 155). Then, as now, the population must have consisted of feral birds, the ubiquitous town pigeon, which often closely resemble the ancestral Rock Pigeon in plumage and nesting habits.]

107 Turtle Dove [European Turtle Dove *Streptopelia turtur*]
I have heard of its breeding in our neighbourhood.
[Breeding has rarely, if ever, been confirmed in Cornwall, though it may have occurred in 1977, 1978 and 1981. In 1821, Couch was "inform'd on good Authority, that turtle doves frequent the neighbourhood of Portallow {in Talland} every summer" (iii, 98), but this may only indicate birds of passage at the height of the spring migration, as on on 12 May 1847 "shot in the Townplace at Talland; supposedly newly arrived" (ix, 114). Clement Jackson presented to Truro Museum in 1841 a "Young" Turtle Dove shot at Looe, but again this is no proof of the nesting of a species he only knew of "in spring and autumn" (*MNH*, 1830, p. 176). Couch first noted one in his possession "shot in this neighbourhood", 30 September 1820 (iii, 87).]

108 Wood Pidgeon [Stock Pigeon *Columba oenas*]

[Considering the remarks by Eyton and Bewick quoted above under Rock Pigeon, it is not surprising that Couch gave no information other than the scientific name *C. oenas*, now given to the Stock Dove or Stock Pigeon as it is offically called. In 1838, Couch described the Stock Dove as "Not common". Its status has not changed because it remains an uncommon breeding bird largely confined to east Cornwall.

Why there should have been such confusion about the various species of pigeon is uncertain, particulary as Gilbert White, in his letter of 30 November 1780, clearly saw the difference between the Stock Dove and Wood Pigeon. John Ray (1678, p. 185 and Plate XXXV) used the name "Ring-Dove" for what is evidently the Wood Pigeon, and "Stock-Dove or Wood-Pigeon" for the Stock Dove, but knew that they were different species.]

Wood Pigeon (top) and Stock Dove, after Ray

Gallinaceous Birds

109 Partridge [Grey Partridge *Perdix perdix*]

Common. [Added later] I have been inform'd of its landing on our coast, from seaward, in a flock.

[In 1832, Richard Barrett reported that in August or early September, when he and others were out seining at Whitsand Bay, they saw 200 "coming in from the Sea, so far as his Eye could reach, & they approach'd & flew but just over the Boats, landed on the grass and ran about in the usual way of the Birds. He saw them clearly, & had no doubt of the Species; & that they had come across the Sea" (vi, 24). This is an unusual observation if true and not wrongly identified Quails. West European Partridges are not migratory, though they may feed locally on dunes and coastal shingle. Partridges were universally distributed in the 19th century but are now scarce breeding birds in east Cornwall.

In 1867, Thomas Couch told Jonathan that at Roscarrock (St Endellion) "Mr Mark Guy observed a brood of 12 young Partridges in the first week in January - they appeared to be about a month old" (xii, 27). For a species that breeds in about May, this is an error and relates to the fact that coveys (family parties) remain together until the following January or February. Thus in 1830, J. Thompson informed Couch "that he has seen so many as 20 young ones in Company with the old pair, all of one size & keeping together" (v, 136). In 1835, Richard Widger reported that on one occasion "he found 22 eggs in one nest" (vi, 158), a not unusual number as up to 40 have been recorded.]

110 Quail [Common Quail *Coturnix coturnix*]

It sometimes remains thro' the Winter. [Added later] Quail from its stooping, or cowering, on appearance of danger, as signifying quell.

[In January 1816, G. Rundle told Couch that "he had seen a flock of Quails, this winter. They commonly keep in companies of 7 or 8, but are somewhat rare. He says he has seen them in Summer, & that some were bred on Wealand {Wayland, Pelynt} estate - of this I am not a judge" (i, 87). Couch reported one killed on 11 November 1848 (ix, 157). In the summer of 1847, the Quail was "unusually plentiful...heard in many fields, but not seen, from its habit of hiding" (ix, 121). The Quail is now a scarce summer visitor, but when it was more abundant in Britain winter records were not unusual, though more particularly in Ireland.

Quail is from the Old French *quaille* (now *caille*), rendered "quale" by William Turner in 1544.]

111 Black Grouse [*Tetrao tetrix*]

One was kill'd at Wadebridge in the Winter of 1820-1. It was formerly common.

[The Wadebridge bird was presumably female since Couch called it a "Black hen" (iii, 99). In 1690, the "Heath Poult" was considered fair game on the Trebartha estate, North Hill, but became progressively scarcer on Bodmin Moor where breeding was last proved in 1904. Hybrids between this and a male Pheasant were not unknown: the gamekeeper of E. H. Rodd's father at Trebartha Hall killed one on the moor nearby in mid-October 1838, and another had been received "some years since" by Mr Drew of Devonport from Sir W. Call, "killed no doubt on the same range of moors" (*RRIC*, 1838, p. 39).]

112 Corn Crake [*Crex crex*]

Common in Summer. One was shot on West Looe Down Decr. 24, after frost & snow, perhaps from being wounded, as I know was the case in another instance of this Bird staying late.

[The above record was of a bird shot by G. Rundle in 1815 (i, 88), the first of several noted by Couch: 22 October 1818, 30 November 1820 and 27 October 1824 (ii, 151; iii, 89; iv 67). On 5 February 1852, he examined one killed near Portallow, Talland, "another proof that this bird does not always migrate" (x, 40). A remarkable migration occurred on Scilly in the autumn of 1857 when "fifteen to twenty couple were killed by a single gun" on the higher moors, St. Mary's (*RRIC*, 1857, p. 20). Yarrell noted that the species had sometimes been shot in winter in mistake for Woodcock, especially in the west of Ireland. The breeding population of this once widespread British bird is now largely confined to the Western Isles of Scotland.]

113 Spotted Rail [Spotted Crake *Porzana porzana*]

Rare.

[Mr James of St Keverne shot two sometime before 1808 (*MM*, 1809, p. 527). Nicholas Hare obtained a bird "lately shot" in the vicinity of Dozmary Pool, St Neot, in 1846 (*WB*, 6 xi 1846; *Pz*, 1848, p. 211). Most records are of migrants, as one "shot at Swanpool {Falmouth} last week by Mr W. May" (*WB*, 5 x 1849). F. R. Rodd was the first to see young of this secretive breeding bird at Crowdy Marsh, Davidstow, in June 1860 (F. R.'s annotation in his copy of E. H. Rodd, 1864). They bred here again in 1862 and near Dozmary Pool in 1874.]

114 Water Rail [*Rallus aquaticus*]

Common & stationary: but of retiring habits: running into an hole when alarm'd. It is rarely seen with us, but in Winter.

[Breeding is difficult to prove, but may well be annual in Cornwall. Migrants and winter visitors are widespread. Couch recorded two migrants at sea. The first "As John Minards was on his return from America, when entering the Chops of the {English} Channel, end of September {1834} a Water rail flew on board the Ship & was taken", as was a Chaffinch a few days before (vi, 146). The second, on 12 May 1849, flew into the sail of a local fishing boat and was picked up dead from the sea (ix, 166, 168).]

115 Olivaceous Gallinule [Little Crake *Porzana parva*]

Rare.

Little Crake, after Bewick

[At the beginning of 1821, Couch described a "gallinule" with light green legs and chestnut body, its dusky yellow bill shorter than the length of its head, quill feathers of the wing edged with white, breast a deep dusk, but chin and belly lighter and whitish under the tail. He did not mention any barred plumage, nor stated where it had been obtained, but thought it was the *Gallinula Foljambei* of Bewick (iii, 97-99). The first confirmed Cornish record of this rare migrant from the Continent was killed by Augustus Pechell on Scilly in the early 1850s (Clark & Rodd, 1906, p. 24).]

116 Water Hen [Common Moorhen *Gallinula chloropus*]

Common, but local.

On 24 May 1845, Couch recorded that "Some time since a Bird was seen on our River, that was suspected to be a Coot, & now a Nest has been found, on the mud, on the upper border of the millpool, that belongs to the same Bird". He added later, "probably a Water Hen" (ix, 16). The locality would not have been congenial to Coots.]

117 Coot [Common Coot *Fulica atra*]

Common. There seems to be no doubt that our Species is different from F. atra Bewick's Br. Birds Vol. 2 p129, in as much as I never saw it with the Spot under the Eye.

Coot, after Bewick

[A small half-circular streak of white below the eye is much more inconspicuous than indicated by Bewick's engraving and is hardly visible in the field. Couch examined a specimen that proved the point on 11 November 1826, "taken in a pool among the Rocks" (iv, 154). He gave more information about its local distribution on 8 November 1832 (vi, 35): "A Coot was shot in the moist ground on Penillick Estate {Pennellick, Pelynt}. This Bird is never seen in our neighbourhood in Summer; a circumstance that can scarcely altogether depend on its habits of concealment. That at least they do change quarters & as this seems on appearance from the fact that on the day before the above named Bird was shot, another was caught at West Looe, where it flew over an hedge, & pitch'd on an apple tree, where it continued a short time. The time it thus alight'd was a little before daybreak; which shows the season of emigration."

Coots were uncommon winter visitors to Cornwall in Couch's day, only becoming more widespread with proof of nesting late in the century. In 1853, Couch noted that "near Penzance the Coot is found in the Summer; altho' with us it is seen only in Winter" (x, 162), so it may have bred then at Marazon Marsh.]

118 Little Bustard [*Tetrax tetrax*]

A specimen was shot on Berry down Sepr. 23, 1831, its weight 1 lb 14 oz, length from bill to tail 18 in, to toes 19 in, expanse 2 ft 11 in: on dissection it prov'd to be a male, tho' in plumage describ'd as female: that is as figur'd by Bewick, without a black neck or band of white.

[This specimen, an adult male in winter plumage, survives in Plymouth City Museum. Details pasted on the back of the case reveal that it was shot by John Lean and "having been brought to me while warm there can be no doubt of the fact. Richard Buller, Rector of Lanreath". There are two Berry Downs, the one in St Neot being closer to Lanreath than the one in Sheviock. Buller gave the bird to Clement Jackson who stuffed it (v, 164). "Seven or eight of these Birds were killed by different persons, in the Land's End District, in the month of December {1853}. Two of them were exhibited together in a poultry shop in Penzance, in the last week of the month" (x, 179). This was a remarkable influx. Rodd obtained a female on 22 November and may be the bird from St Just-in-Penwith engraved by J. T. Blight in his *A Week at The Land's End*, 1861, p. 174).]

Little Bustard, after Blight

Plovers & Sand Pipers

119 Great Plover [Stone-curlew *Burhinus oedicnemus*]

According to Montagu this Bird has been seen in Cornwall. One shot at Morval Decr. 31, 1830.

[Clement Jackson probably stuffed the bird shot at Morval (v, 164). Montagu stated that it is "not frequent so far west as Devonshire, and still more rare in Cornwall". Nevertheless, records date back to Ray (1678, p. 293): "Mr Willughby acknowledges a third sort of *Godwit*, which in *Cornwall* they call the Stone-Curlew, differing from the precedent in that it hath a much shorter and slenderer Bill than either of them." Mr Trembath of Mayon, Sennen, shot one "near the Land's End" on 20 December 1850 (*WB*, 27 xii).]

120 Golden Plover [European Golden Plover *Pluvialis apricaria*]

Common, breeding in high grounds; but only descending to the Coast in Winter.

[There is no proof that the Golden Plover has bred closer to Cornwall than on Dartmoor. Edward Moore (1830, p. 321) noted that "A brood of six was obtained on the banks of the Tamar, in 1827", but Moore usually meant by "brood" a small party because he used the same word to describe the Turnstone that has not been proved to breed anywhere in Britain.]

121 Lapwing [Northern Lapwing *Vanellus vanellus*]

A winter visitant. It is term'd Horniwink with us. [Added later] It breeds in Cornwall.

[Lapwings nested on most of the Cornish Moors throughout the 19th century, but is now a scarce breeeder. What would now be called a "weather movement" was recorded by Couch on 24 February 1831: "This morning about 10 o'clock were seen coming from the Southward by our fishermen, who were then 3 or 4 miles from land; about twenty to thirty of these Birds. They came straight to the land, & in their judgment seemed fatigued with flying" (v, 149). Dialect "horniwink" alludes to the bird's horn-like crest feathers.]

122 Ring Plover [Great Ringed Plover *Charadrius hiaticula*]

Common on the Shore thro' the Year, in retir'd places.

[In the 19th century it nested widely on shingle beaches, even on Eastern Green, Penzance, until as recently as 1922. Human pressure has since confined them to Scilly where they have also declined in numbers. Couch was taken a specimen on 29 December 1829 "during hard frost & snow: thus in another instance shewing this Bird stays with us thro' the Winter" (v, 102). C. W. Peach shot on 22 February 1836 a "Sand Lark ... nearly all white" which had frequented the beach at Caerhays for several months" (*WB*, 11 iii).]

123 Grey Plover [*Pluvialis squatarola*]

[Couch makes no comment, nor in his 1838 account, about this regular migrant and winter visitor that does not appear in the large flocks characteristic of the Golden Plover. On 26 January 1842, he noted that Clement Jackson had obtained a Grey Plover a few days before, "the first for several years" (viii, 240). Couch called it "very scarce with us" when, in February 1862, Stephen Clogg of Looe had one in his possession "caught not far off" (x, 527). Couch must have seen migrants at Looe in May and August 1816. His descriptions of unidentified waders fit well; the size of a plover, geyish or brownish above, white beneath and "thro' the glass, a rim of white on their {wings'} inner edge ... they were looking for food on the rocks and beach, but did not appear to wade, & when on the wing had a sound like whistling" (ii, 4, 30-31).]

124 Sanderling [*Calidris alba*]

Scarce. My friend Mr C. Jackson observes that he has seen two matured Specimens shot at Swanpool near Falmouth; & he once found a small flock immatured at the same place.

[Sanderlings are by no means scarce as passage migrants and winter visitors. In August 1816, there were "plenty of Sanderlings on Looe Island" (ii, 31). Jackson's "matured" birds may mean they were in full breeding plumage, not commonly seen in Cornwall. Ray "saw many of them on the Sea-coasts of Cornwall" during his visit of 1662, noting that about Penzance it was also called *Curwillet*, a dialect name derived from its shrill call when disturbed (Ray, 1678, p. 303).]

125 Red Sandpiper [Red Knot *Calidris canutus*]

Two specimens were purchased in Falmouth Market in April 1822.

[See also the next but one entry.]

126 Reeve [Ruff *Philomachus pugnax*]

Very rare. A specimen of the Reeve was killed near Truro, March 1829 [*MNH*, 1830, p. 176].

[The Ruff, female Reeve, is a regular passage migrant and rare winter resident on Cornish estuaries. The male is occasionally seen beginning to acquire its impressive summer plumage. One "in the midst of change" was killed near Looe on 3 April 1845, Couch's only *Journal* record (ix, 10).]

127 Knot [Red Knot *Calidris canutus*]

A few in Winter.

Red Sandpiper (winter) and right, Knot (breeding plumage), after Bewick

[Couch followed Bewick in assuming the Red Sandpiper and Knot were different species, but when he published his 1838 account he appreciated that they were the same. Two "Red Knots" shot at Lansallos were taken to him on 3 October 1834 (vi, 96). Red Knot originally described the breeding plumage. The species is a regular, if rather scarce, migrant and winter visitor to Cornish estuaries.]

128 Green Sandpiper [*Tringa ochropus*]

A specimen was kill'd at Stythians [Stithians], August 6, 1824.

[The bird was in in Clement Jackson's collection (v, 74). Another was killed at Paramoor, St Ewe, the same year (*MNH*, 1830, p. 176). August is the main month for seeing this migrant, usually in ones or twos at freshwater sites. Clement Jackson shot a pair at a small pond near St Keyne on 14 August 1851, probably one of the ponds just west of the village at East Trevillies (*TN*, 1851, p. 212).]

129 Common Sandpiper [*Actitis hypoleucos*]

[Couch made no comment, but in his 1838 account described it as "Not uncommon". In his day, it bred annually on Bodmin Moor (Nicholas Hare, *Pz*, 1848, pp. 211-12). They favoured the deserted tin streamworks and sand-banks (F. R. Rodd's annotated E. H. Rodd, 1864). It probably nested there in 1988 for the first time since 1910.]

130 Dunlin Purr [Dunlin *Calidris alpina*]

[Couch made no comment, but in his 1838 account described it as "Rather scarce", which it was as a breeding bird on Bodmin Moor. Nicholas Hare was the first to obtain eggs from a nest on Goodaver Downs adjoining Dozmary Pool, St Neot. They had been found in the last week of May 1848 by a farmer's boy who told him that the "stark" only bred "with them occasionally, and that a pair or two is the most he has seen in any one year" (*Pz*, 1848, p. 211). Not one was seen the following year (*Pz*, 1849, p. 316). "Stark" is an otherwise unrecorded dialect name.

As a migrant and winter visitor, the Dunlin is the commonest of all small waders. "Purr(e)" (derived from its trilling call) was a widespread dialect name for this species in its winter plumage. Montagu (1802), who found Dunlins "Not uncommon on the Devonshire and Cornwall coast", was the first to realise that the "purre" was the same species.]

131 Pigmy Curlew [Curlew Sandpiper *Calidris ferruginea*]

Not uncommon at Swanpool near Falmouth, where several have been kill'd; on the authority of Mr C. Jackson.

[Clement Jackson shot the first on 1 October 1823 and four in September 1824 (v, 74). It is a regular migrant with Dunlins, common in some autumns, rare in others. R. J. Julian reported a flock of nearly 40 on the Lynher estuary in September-October 1850 (*TN*, 1851, p. 59).]

132 Purple Sandpiper [*Calidris maritima*]

[Couch made no comment, but in his 1838 account described it as "Not uncommon", perhaps because one of its regular winter quarters has long been the foreshore at Hannafore, Looe. Clement Jackson seemed "to have no doubt", in 1832, "that the Selninger Piper of Bewick" is the Knot (vi, 22). The name was Pennant's and Bewick's for the Purple Sandpiper.]

133 Little Stint [*Calidris minuta*]

Mr C. Jackson informs me "I have several times shot this Species at Swanpool [Falmouth] singly; but I once saw a small flock of 10 or 12 there. I have also found it in company with the Purr". The bill & Legs of this Species [Dunlin] sufficiently distinguish it from T. minuta [Little Stint], being much stouter; and dusky black.

[The Little Stint is a more common autumn migrant in some years than in others, but is generally scarce. J. C. Bellamy (1830, p. 212) knew of specimens shot on the Tamar in August and September.]

134 Least Sandpiper [Temminck's Stint *Calidris temminckii*]

Mr Jackson says "I have shot a Specimen of this scarce Species at Swanpool [Falmouth] Sept. 11, 1822, & have seen one shot there since, which only differs from the former in being of a lighter colour." It differs materially from the little stint, the bill & legs being shorter & more slender, & of a pale brownish green, the colour being the same as in the common Sandpiper.

[Jackson's specimens are the first Cornish records.]

135 Turnstone [Ruddy Turnstone *Arenaria interpres*]

Tringa interpres *and* T. morinella, *after Bewick*

[Couch made no comment, but in his 1838 account described it as "Not uncommon". In June 1832 (vi, 22), from three specimens in Clement Jackson's collection, Couch correctly concluded that Bewick's *Tringa morinella* and *T. interpres* were the same species in different states of plumage, having already described one he saw on Looe Island on 19 May 1830 (v, 125).]

136 Oyster Catcher [Eurasian Oystercatcher *Haematopus ostralegus*]

Scarce.

[In December 1815 (i, 80), Couch was told that "Sea Pies" were "in plenty on Looe Island". In 1822 (*IM*, p. 711) he only included it amongst the regular winter visitors. There is evidence to suggest that breeding was then confined to Scilly and only extended to the mainland from about 1870. Edward Moore (1830, p. 322), in his account of the birds of south Devon, made no mention of breeding, describing it as "Not uncommon near the sea shores in small flocks, in winter".]

137 Grey Phalarope [*Phalaropus fulicarius*]

It comes in winter, sometimes in considerable number[s]. For its habits see Loudon's Magazine of Nat. Hist. Vol, [3, 1830, p.177]. Mr Jackson is convinced that this and the Red Phalarope are the same: which is confirm'd to me by Mr Yarrell, who says that he convinc'd Mr Bewick of the same fact, by showing him Specimens in all the intermediate stages of colour (*J*, vii, 2-3).]

Grey Phalarope, after Yarrell

[Couch includes a thumb-nail sketch of a phalarope that, from the shorter, thicker bill, has to be the Grey. Red Phalarope was an alternative name also used for the Red-necked Phalarope *P. lobatus*, both species being confused in winter pluamge. Yarrell (1843) fully realized that there were two species. The Grey Phalarope is the more common and an annual visitor, though rarely appearing in huge flocks. Clement Jackson found them to be abundant in January 1829 (v, 61) and received at least 21 specimens in October 1831 when heavy SSW gales drove in large flocks, "at least from Looe to Fowey; ten were kill'd out of one flock that consisted of about fifty" (v, 167). Dr Edward Moore also wrote (*MM*, 1837, p. 322) of large numbers in October 1831 when a dead Rorqual whale, discovered off Plymouth harbour, was towed into the Sound and stranded on the beach. "It swarmed with sea birds, notably the Grey Phalarope which frequented the river for two to three weeks and many were shot. Mr Drew had over 90 specimens, Pincombe 30 to 40, and Bolitho as many." Moore (1830, p. 329) had also noted one shot on the Cornish side of the Tamar at St John's Lake after hard south-west winds on 6-8 October 1828.

The 1830 account by Couch, Jackson & Lakes reads "not uncommon on the coast in winter, but their habits make them seem so rare. They never perch on rocks or on the sands; but alight on the water with ease, and are capable of swimming against a rapid tide. Not shy." Large numbers were again abundant at the end of November and early December 1835, "& when swimming the little alarm they felt at being shot at was surprising. It seems certain that they visit us at this Season every Year" (vii, 47). Phalaropes are the most pelagic of the waders. Their lobed feet facilitate swimming and their characteristic habit of pirouetting in the water, as Couch described on 6 October 1846; "they continued with us until within a day or two" of the 27th (ix, 99, 101).

When Couch visited the Polytechnic Hall, Falmouth, in September 1853, he saw a Red-necked Phalarope "caught at Falmouth in this month" (x, 163), but never seems to have received an example himself.]

The Woodcock Kind

138 Woodcock [Eurasian Woodcock *Scolopax rusticola*]

Abundant in Winter. Instances of its remaining thro' the Summer are not uncommon, probably from having been wounded, & thus render'd incapable of distant flight. The instance mention'd by Borlase seems to be the only authentic one of its having bred here [see Borlase's Plate XXIV, fig XII in the Introduction.]

[The Revd William Borlase recorded the discovery of a nest with two eggs in the summer of 1755 in the neighbourhood of Penzance (1758, p. 245). Couch wrote that "in the first week in June, 1843, a young Woodcock was sent to Mr C. Jackson, for preservation, that was found on the public road near Bodmin, and when discovered it was scarcely dead. As it was not of age for distant flight, it was judged to have been dropped where found, by the parents; which have been supposed to be in the habit of carrying their young to their feeding places, before they have acquired sufficient strength to convey themselves" (viii, 308; *Supplement*, 1844, pp. 147-148). This curious habit was only authenticated in the 1940s. The 1843 bird was found on 7 June by the guard of the coach *Telegraph* on the turnpike between St Austell and Liskeard (*Pz*, 1846, p. 33). In 1849, "Towards the end of June a young Woodcock was knock'd down near Boconnoc & a pair of Birds often seen near the spot" (ix, 179). Another "seen several times within the last fortnight" was shot on 11 June 1839 at Bodwannick Wood, Lanivet, but without any proof that it had attempted to nest (*WB*, 14 vi). Woodcocks have rarely been proved to breed in Cornwall in spite of a national spread in their range from about the 1830s.

Most *Journal* entries consist of the arrival dates of birds in autumn, the "early Woodcock" having always been much prized by local sportsmen, as one shot by Harold Billing on 24 September 1832 (vi, 33). Early in November 1809, "a woodcock walk'd deliberately into the house of Jane Johns, at Polperro, & was taken alive & unhurt. He was placed in a Cage & sent to Plymouth. Woodcocks were at that time scarce" (i, 2).]

139 Snipe [Common Snipe *Gallinago gallinago*]
It breeds in our Moors.

[It still does on Bodmin Moor, though the characteristic drumming sound of the displaying male is now a far less familiar sound. Wintering birds remain widespread. Common Snipes exhibit much variation in plumage, notably the melanistic "Sabine's Snipe" originally believed to be a distinct species. E. H. Rodd thought he had one in his collection that had been killed about Christmas time in 1805 on Lanyon Moor, Madron, but Yarrell did not agree, though the bird had a darker and more somber spotted appearance than the normal form (*RRIC*, 1838, pp. 38-9). Couch noted an undoubted example that had been shot near Carnanton, St Mawgan-in-Pydar, in January 1862 (x, 525; *RCG*, 24 i; Rodd, 1864, p. 27.)

A large flock of Snipe on 6 May 1850 at Pendeen, St Just-in-Penwith, was seen "by many persons who were on the road at the time of their flight" after a period of very stormy weather (ix, 193; *RCG*, 10 v). This is an unusually late date for migrants.]

140 Jack Snipe [*Lymnocryptes minimus*]
Common in Winter.

[This is an uncommon migrant and winter visitor that was apparently more numerous in the 19th century; W. P. Cocks called it "not uncommon" (*TN*, 1851, p. 137). In January 1848, Mr Coath of Raphael, Lansallos, brought Couch a "Jack Snipe, kill'd the 6th Inst., the first he has seen for the season; but he has heard of one or two others a day or two before: the weather mild" (ix, 138).]

141 Godwit [Bar-tailed Godwit *Limosa lapponica*]
[Couch made no comment, but his use of the old scientific name *Scolopax aegocephala* indicates the Bar-tailed Godwit in winter plumage as figured by Bewick. This, and the Black-tailed Godwit *L. limosa* were confused by early writers (see below under "Red-breasted Snipe" 148 for fuller details). Couch was well aware of the differences, and in 1836 (vii, 66-68) he described a dead "Barr'd Godwit", well advanced in summer plumage, taken on board a fishing boat nine leagues from Polperro on 11 May, "& another man informs me that about 10 leagues off, hundreds of these birds were seen,

Bar-tailed Godwit, after Bewick

in flocks, flying from the West Eastwards". The Black-tailed Godwit was generally much more rare, Couch noting that one had been taken in 1849 (ix, 179), evidently the bird shot by Pechell on Scilly (*Pz*, 1849, p. 271).]

142 Great Snipe [*Gallinago media*]
[Inserted later] I have ascertain'd its being kill'd in Cornwall.
[One was shot near Marazion about 12 March 1839, the first record for Cornwall (viii, 29; *WB*, 15 iii). Another was killed at Gyllingvase Marsh, Falmouth, in December 1848 (W. P. Cocks, *TN*, 1851, p.137). Records of this vagrant, sometimes called the Great Plover or Solitary Snipe, were more numerous in the 19th century. Couch noted (x, 274) one recorded by E. H. Rodd. This was an immature bird killed by Mr Holland the Trevethoe gamekeeper at Cold Harbour Moor, Towednack, in the first week of October 1855. Another was seen by him "in the same locality" (*RCG*, 12 x). Another was killed near Liskeard in September 1859 (*RCG*, 23 ix).]

143 Green Shank [Common Greenshank *Tringa nebularia*]
In Winter, rare.
[Couch described in detail one taken to him on 2 October 1822 (iii, 150). It is a regular passage migrant and winter visitor to our estuaries, and probably no more uncommon in Couch's day than now.]

144 Redshank [Common Redshank *Tringa totanus*]
In Winter, rare.

[Rare it may have been in Polperro harbour, and Couch only recorded one, a female that Clement Jackson had shot on 4 April 1845 at Terras on the East Looe River (ix, 12), though it was not uncommon in his day. Nowadays it is one of the commonest migrants and winter visitors to estuaries, but there is some evidence that it became more numerous in the last quarter of the 19th century. A pair nested on Bodmin Moor in 1904.]

145 Curlew [Eurasian Curlew *Numenius arquata*]
Common, but nocturnal.

[Couch's "nocturnal" is probably intended to mean that its habits depend on the state of the tide, hence it feeds on uncovered mud flats by day or night. His comment stems from December 1815 when he was told that Curlews were common on Looe Island at night (i, 80, 96), "flying about & whistling by moonlight". His 1838 account is more accurate: "In Winter; and a few remain to breed in the high grounds". They reguarly nested on most of the moors throughout the 19th century, though few do so now.

The stomachs of Curlews, shot on the "beach of the Looe River" on 3 March 1828, contained "many black beetles; hooks baited with them would be a good method of taking them" (v, 28). The insects must have been eaten inland where adult and larval beetles form part of their varied diet.]

146 Whimbrel [*Numenius phaeopus*]
It arrives here in flocks in May, & is call'd the May Bird. [Added later] Our fishermen see them in Mid Channel, crossing from France.

[Couch visited Looe Island on 19 May 1830 and saw a Whimbrel shot (v, 130). On 25 May 1832, he wrote that "some of the fishermen inform me they have seen them yesterday the 24th at 10 leagues S of the Deadman {Dodman Point} at 4 O'clock in the afternoon; & that they often hear them in the night. They call them Curlews; but they know two sorts & say these are the smaller kind. One flew round the Boat several times" (vi, 21). Whimbrels may have been the birds seen on 11 May 1838 by Thomas Holten: "large flocks of Curlews, or Whimbrels, flying north-east - he thinks they might have been thousands" (vii, 284).]

147 Avoset [Pied Avocet *Recurvirostra avosetta*]
This Bird has been seen near the Swanpool [Falmouth], & there is a Specimen in the museum at Truro, shot near the same place.

[An Avocet was presented to the Museum between 1824 and 1829 by Capt. Jenkins, and another between 27 August 1831 and 29 November 1832 by E. W. Pendarves. No details were given about the origin of either, but the Swanpool bird was seen before 1830 (*MNH*, 1830, p. 177). W. P. Cocks (*TN*, 1851, p. 114) noted that one shot at Swanpool in November 1845 was "the second in the locality within the last ten years". Edward Moore (1830, p. 331) also knew of one shot on the Tamar. Avocets bred in eastern England until 1843, but did not do so again until 1946. Since then, wintering numbers have gradually increased in the south-west with 422 counted on the Lynher-St John's Lake-Tamar complex in January 1999.]

148 Redbreasted Snipe [Bar-tailed Godwit *Limosa lapponica*]
Montagu thinks he has seen this Bird in a Collection in Cornwall. (It should have been placed after the Redshank).

[Couch's English name and his scientific name *Scolopax noveboracensis* were used by Montagu (1813) for the Bar-tailed Godwit attaining its breeding plumage: "In a small collection of birds belonging to a medical gentleman at Marazion, in Cornwall, we recollect noticing a bird very much mutilated by insects, that was supposed to be the Red Godwit {Black-tailed Godwit}, but we now have very little doubt that it was of this species" {Bar-tailed Godwit}. The name Red Godwit *Scolopax lapponica* was used by Montagu in 1803 for the Black-tailed Godwit. In breeding plumage, the Black-tailed has a chestnut neck and breast, while the Bar-tailed has all the underparts and neck chestnut. Little wonder there was much confusion over identification, even though the Black-tailed is easily identified in flight by its white wing-bar and black-and-white tail pattern. Both species are passage migrants and winter visitors to Cornwall.]

Heron tribe

149 Crane [Common Crane *Grus grus*]

A specimen in the Collection of Mr Drew of Devonport was kill'd in Cornwall in 1827-8. I think I have heard of another Specimen kill'd in the County.

[The bird in Drew's collection frequented the banks of the Tamar in September 1826 (not 1827-8) and was shot on the Devon side near Buckland Monachorum (Moore, *TPI*, 1830, p. 322). An earlier bird was noted by Couch (iii, 49) on 4 January 1820, shot by John Hocken (probably of Penhellick, St Pinnock) "a few days since ... in a brake, which from the description I have receiv'd appears to be a Crane. From the head to its feet it was four feet nine inches long."]

150 Heron [Grey Heron *Ardea cinerea*]

Common.

[Couch's first entry is for 1848 (ix, 144): "Mrs Harding, of Trelawny {Trelawne, Pelynt}, informs me that she well remembers when her brother - Sir William T{relawny} lived at Penquite, on the west bank of the Fowey River, that on that side, opposite the ford, there was a heronry, of many Nests, in a tree or trees - either on the Penquite Estate, or a little below it. It seems to have been there long, & now I have enquir'd by Mr Peach, of Fowey; who informs me that it is there still. I shall search out more about it: but it is the only one I have heard of in Cornwall - & the long attachment to one place is not the least curious part of the circumstance." C. W. Peach, the Fowey landing waiter best known as an amateur geologist, wrote to Couch on Monday 16 May 1848 to arrange the trip in his boat after 4 p.m. on the Thursday or Friday. Fidelity of heronries to one place is well known, though sites may move. In another letter about the same time, Peach said that "the greater part of the herons have left their old abode at Penquite and have founded a Colony nearer Ethy. Still a few linger at the old spot." The new site is in the same area as the present colony on the east bank of the Fowey in St Winnow parish. Peach was also told by Mrs Tweedy of a "Heronry at Philleigh on the Fal". This must be the site still occupied by about four nests in Borlase Wood in Philleigh parish and marked on the 25 inch O.S. map surveyed in 1878.

Clement Jackson first drew Couch's attention to birds breeding on the East Looe River when in about June 1848 "a young Heron scarcely enough fledg'd to fly, was found, just then dead, in a Brake at Morval" (ix, 147). The site was soon found; a "few nests of Herons, for the first time, in a tree on the Trenant Estate {Duloe}, on the East branch of the Looe River - nearly opposite the place where the crossing place is. This year, I saw them & am inform'd there are about five Nests. They are on the tops of the trees; & Mr Peel is determin'd to protect them" (ix, 164). This heronry is now at the junction of the East and West Looe Rivers with an average of nine nests, the same as at St Winnow. Cornish heronries rarely contain more than twenty nests.]

151 Purple Heron [*Ardea purpurea*]

A specimen of this rare Species came to my hands May 3, 1822 [*J*, iii, 137-8], of which an account was sent to Mr Bewick; & was publish'd by him in the last Edition of his History of British Birds. This was the first publish'd notice of this Bird as a British Species, but Col. Montagu had met with it before.

Purple Heron, after Bewick

Couch's drawing of a Purple Heron

[Couch includes a pen-and-ink sketch of the Purple Heron. Bewick (1826, Addenda, 410-412) took his illustration from an undated specimen lent to him by the Revd Keir Vaughan, rector of Aveton Gifford, and may have been the specimen that J. C. Bellamy reported had "been obtained on the Tamar" (1839, p. 210). Bewick acknowledged that he was "favoured ... with a coloured drawing of a bird, which is supposed to be of the same species as the foregoing. Mr Couch says, 'it alighted on a fishing boat, two or three leagues from land, May 3d, 1822, and was taken: when brought on shore it soon died'." Following a long description of the bird, Bewick continues, "It has been judged proper to figure this bird, with the abrupt bend in the neck, as it appears in Mr Couch's drawing, which was taken while the bird was fresh and in full feather, and our figure, for this reason, has been somewhat more fully feathered than the stuffed specimen, which appeared to be much dried and shrivelled". Couch's pencil and wash drawing sent to Thomas Bewick survives in the Hancock Museum, Newcastle-upon-Tyne. Couch was unable to identify his specimen until April 1824 when he visited the British Museum and examined Montagu's "African Heron" as he had called it (iv, 22). Montagu referred to an undated specimen shot at Ashdown Park, near Lambourne, Berkshire, but had not seen one in Cornwall.]

152 Little Bittern [*Ixobrychus minutus*]

A Specimen shot at Mawgan in Cornwall. May 19, 1832.

[The specimen was shot by Michael Cayzer of Moreland (now Merlin farm), St Mawgan-in-Pydar, and presented to Truro Museum (*WB*, 25 v), but the specimen no longer exists. It must have been at the Museum that Couch saw it (vi, 21). Stephen Clogg of Looe showed Couch "a very pretty specimen of the little Bittern, which however was shot, near Looe - so long ago as last May" 1858 (x, 418).]

153 Black Stork [*Ciconia nigra*]

[This was inserted later without comment, but in 1838 Couch wrote that "One Specimen only is known to have been kill'd in Cornwall, on the borders of the Tamar". This was the second British occurrence, shot on 5 November 1831, probably on Beggar's Island in the Lynher estuary. It went into the collection of Mr Drew of Plymouth before passing to E. H. Rodd (vi, 25; D'Urban & Mathew, 1892, p. 197).]

154 Egrett [Little Egret *Egretta garzetta*]

Two Specimens were shot near Penzance in April 1824, one of which is in the Collection of Mr John of that place.

[This was an error that Couch noted with an insert at the bottom of the page (see Squacco Heron,

157), though not before Yarrell published the record in his *British Birds* (1843, Vol. II, p. 459). Under Egret in his 1838 account, Couch acknowledged his mistake, but also added, "One or two Specimens are known". The latter may be the pair recorded by Henry Mewburn of St Germans in a letter dated 7 March 1826, taken in Cornwall "within the last eighteen months" (G. T. Fox, 1827, pp. 252-255). However, it is more than likely that Mewburn had also been wrongly informed about the identity of the Penzance birds. Had the egrets been seen on the Tamar or elsewhere in his home territory, Mewburn would have been more specific about the occurrence, and it is significant that Edward Moore does not mention the species in "The Ornithology of South Devon" (*TPI*, 1830). The "One or two on the Tamar" noted much later by J. Brooking Rowe, without dates (*TPI*, 1862-63), presumably relate to Mewburn's supposed birds.

E. H. Rodd (*Pz*, 1850, p. 418) had not heard of any Cornish example. However, an egret was reported to have been shot near Grampound about mid-May 1848 by Mr Passmore, the Truro taxidermist (ix 145; *RCG*, 19 v). If correct, it is the only record until one wintered at the Hayle estuary from November 1943 until 10 February 1944. Since the 1980s, Little Egrets have become common in southern Britain and have nested in Cornwall and elsewhere. On 14 September 1999, E. Griffiths counted 143 at two roosts on the Cornish side of the Tamar.]

155 Bittern [Great Bittern *Botaurus stellaris*]

Not uncommon.

[The Bittern is more or less an annual winter visitor to marshes such as Marazion. More than usual were reported in January 1838 when five were taken to a Penzance taxidermist. The first noted by Couch was shot on the Looe River in March 1818 by a Mr Were who said it was the second he had known shot in the County (ii, 124). Another was shot at Portwrinkle, Sheviock, in January 1820, though "its wing spread about 7 feet" is over estimated by about three feet (iii, 54). In his 1844 *Supplement*, Couch wrote, "There is no need to record this bird for its rarity; but it seems to abound much more in the west than in the eastern part of the County. But it is here inserted to notice its food. I am assured that in one instance a Red Wing, and in another a Rail was found in its stomach" (viii, 337). Small mammals and birds, swallowed whole, are part of its varied diet. A Bittern and 51 Snipe were shot somewhere in the Penzance area on 25 January 1851 by Mr. Smith, butler to Sir Rose Price of Trengwainton (*WB*, 28 i).]

156 Bay Ibis [Glossy Ibis *Plegadis falcinellus*]

Two specimens were kill'd near Helston, in June 1825, & 2 others at the same time near Penzance.

Glossy Ibis, after Blight

[These are the first Cornish records. J.T. Blight (1861, p. 50) illustrated what is probably Rodd's bird from Tresco shot by Jenkinson on 19 September 1854 (x, 209). Blight also notes another from Paul, clearly one of the two shot "near Penzance" in June 1825 which Courtney (1845, p. 30) said was a poorly preserved specimen from Paul in the possession of Mr Edmonds. The second bird was presented to Truro Museum (v, 75; *MNH*, 1830, p. 177).]

157 Squacco Heron [*Ardeola ralloides*]

What is said above of the Egrett must be applied to this Bird; & the Egrett must be omitted.

[This was the first Cornish occurrence. In his 1838 account, Couch noted that these birds, "formerly supposed to be the Egret, prove to be of this Species". One was shot at Trereife, Madron, and the other seen a few days later at Hayle (*Z*, 1843). More were obtained in May 1849 (ix, 224) when W. H. Vingoe the taxidermist had three killed in the Penzance area, "the most mature" from James Trembath of Mayon, Sennen. About the same time three were taken in St Keverne; "Richard Ivey of Trevenwith has one of the birds alive, and the other two are in the collection of Mr Frederick V. Hill of Helston" (*WB*, 18 & 25 v).]

Divers

158 Crested Grebe [Great Crested Grebe *Podiceps cristatus*]

In its winter plumage this is the Tippet Grebe, C. Urinator. Common on the Coast in winter.

[Bewick believed this to be a different species, calling it Tippet Grebe because the skins, dressed with the feathers on, were made made by furriers into "tippets" worn around the neck and shoulders or as muffs.]

159 Red neck'd Grebe [Red-necked Grebe *Podiceps grisegena*]
Scarce. One Specimen was kill'd in Falmouth harbour, one at Looe, & another at Polperro.

[The Falmouth and Looe specimens were taken before 1830 (*MNH*, p. 177), but Couch does not mention the species in his *Journal*.]

160 Dusky Grebe [Slavonian Grebe *Podiceps auritus*]
In March 1818 I procur'd a Specimen that was shot in the harbour at Polperro, after stormy weather, which had in its stomach a quantity of slender feathers, taken I believe from its own plumage, and swallow'd to allay the sensation of hunger. They were stain'd a bright green colour, by a fluid with which they were saturated.

[Dusky Grebe referred to the winter plumage. Couch was uncertain of its relationship to the "Sclavonian" Grebe, see **162** below.]

161 Ear'd Grebe [Black-necked Grebe *Podiceps nigricollis*]
Bewick has overlook'd this Species, having confounded it with the Sclavonian Grebe (C. Cornatus), as was first pointed out by Montagu, whose accuracy of distinction I am able to confirm by a Comparison of a Specimen of each of these Birds. That one which I examin'd, of the Ear'd Grebe, differ'd however, from Montagu's figure in a few particulars. The figure of Montagu's Bird is too slender, bill too long & slender, the under mandible not sufficiently curv'd thro' its length. The throat black, and not mottled, as in Montagu. It is exceedingly rare. When caught, this Specimen bit with fury, as to break its upper mandible.

[Couch includes a good sketch (see page 118) of the specimen developing its breeding plumage, in which complete state it is uncommon in Cornwall. It was drawn on 1 August from the bird that had "just come into the possession of Clement Jackson" in April 1829 (v, 64, 78). It was a male taken near Truro and presented to Truro Museum (*MNH*, 1830, p. 177), though it no longer survives there. Col. George Montagu's specimen was a male with its plumage "fully matured", shot on 15 March 1811 and sent to him by Col. George Chapman George of Penryn. Until he published his 1813 *Supplement*, Montagu was unclear about the differences between the "Eared" Grebe and the "Sclavonian" or "Horned" Grebe. The only other Black-necked recorded by Couch was shot near Falmouth in a mild but wet and stormy November in 1852 (x, 98).]

Couch's sketch of a Black-necked Grebe

162 Sclavonian Grebe [Slavonian Grebe *Podiceps auritus*]

Rare.

[Rare it always has been in Cornwall in its breeding plumage, but see also under "Dusky Grebe" above. The species was first described as British by Montagu (1802): "This bird, which was rescued from the hands of a fisherman as he was going to pick it, was killed near Truro in Cornwall, on 4th of May, 1796, and presented to me by a friend. It was a male bird, and is now in my museum." Montagu made an error over the year of capture. His MS Diary, preserved in The Natural History Museum, London, clearly states that it was in 1797. The "Horned Grebe", as he called it, was taken to him by a Mr Wych. The only *P. auritus* mentioned by Couch was one he saw in Clement Jackson's collection, killed in November or December 1842 (viii, 293).]

163 Dabchick [Little Grebe *Tachybaptus ruficollis*]

Common.

[Couch added this common species to his list of Cornish birds in May 1816 (ii, 16), "for I suppose this Bird to be what our People call the Dabchick, which frequents lakes & ponds, swims with only its head above water {an exaggeration}, & dives at the flash of a gun, yet will not quit the pond". On 9 March 1818, Couch dissected and described one at length, comparing it to the description given by Ray in 1678 under the name "Colymbus sive Podiceps minor" (ii, 120-123). During the cold January of 1838, a Little Grebe was shot in Polperro harbour, it "div'd & did not rise again. When the tide receded it was found under the bottom of a vessel", but there is no truth in his assumption that this and similar accounts show that shot diving birds submerge to "hide in Crevices" (vii, 268).]

[The following lines of verse complete the bottom of Couch's page. They were probably written after his mother's death on 18 August 1833, a few days short of her ninetieth birthday.]

> Softly we lay
> Our lov'd in death; yet not as death esteem'd
> A gift to be return'd, a pledge redeem'd,
> In God's own day.

164 Great Northern Diver [*Gavia immer*]

Figure in Bewick's Br. Birds Vol. 2 p.170, which however, fails to display the uncommon beauty of its plumage.

Great Northern Diver, after Bewick

A Specimen, not driven by distress of weather, was taken by some fishermen of Polperro, as it lay asleep on the water May 21st, 1823. It liv'd for at least a month in captivity, being carried to the water every day [*J*, iii, 161].

[See also under "Imber" (**166**) below. A flock of seven was seen on the Tamar near Saltash in December 1828, one of which was shot and passed into Edward Moore's collection (*TPI*, 1830, p. 334), while on 17 September 1832, J. C. Bellamy (1839, p. 214-5) saw five off Rame Head, a very early time for migrants. Couch wrote on 8 January 1853: "There are large numbers of Northern Divers - in groups, along our coast - driven perhaps by the long continued stormy weather. Mr Jackson informs me that there were 20 together in Looe roads - I saw 6 or 7 in a group in Talland Sand Bay & Mr Jackson says, the food they were catching was Crabs, not fishes" (x, 111). Crustaceans, molluscs and other marine creatures are commonly eaten, though fish less than a foot long are its main diet.]

165 Speckled Diver [Red-throated Diver *Gavia stellata*]

Common in Winter.

[Bewick (1826) figured a First and a Second Speckled Diver, both assumed to be the young of the Red-throated Diver. Couch used the name Red-throated Diver in 1832 (vi, 8) when one "was shot at Looe, March 15: as it was feeding on Young Mullets. Mr Jackson has no doubt of its being the First Speckled Diver of Bewick, in Summer plumage. The latter is not the Young only, but also the old one in Winter plumage."

Couch does not mention the Black-throated Diver (*Gavia arctica*) which may well have been confused with the other divers. Without close examination, all would have been difficult to separate in winter plumage. See also under Imber (**166**) and Red-throated Diver (**170**).]

Red-throated Diver: "First Speckled Diver", after Bewick

166 Imber [Great Northern Diver *Gavia immer*]

Fleming supposes this to be the immature Bird of the Great Northern Diver; a supposition the more extraordinary, as tho' the latter is exceedingly rare, the Imber is common on our Coast in Winter; and two Specimens remain'd near Looe thro' the whole Summer of 1828.

[John Fleming (1828, p.132) was right and Couch does not mention the Imber in his 1838 account. The name Lesser Imber was used by Bewick for a single specimen subsequently examined by Fleming and identified by him as the Black-throated Diver in non-breeding plumage. Some of Couch's wintering Imbers may well have been the smaller Black-throated Diver. Records of divers remaining throughout the summer are very unusual for Cornwall, though the Great Northern has been recorded in every month of the year.]

167 Foolish Guillemot [Common Guillemot *Uria aalge*]

A summer visitor.

[Couch made several references to "Murs" in his early *Journals* and in his *Illustrations of Instinct* (1847, p. 192). These he regarded as a "kind of Guillemot", but the lack of breeding birds on the south-east coast of Cornwall shows Couch was unfamiliar with the species and its distribution. In 1821 he wrote, "I read in a book that the foolish Guillemot Colymbus Troile, breeds near St Ives in Cornwall" (iii, 131). This was probably in Ray (1678, p. 325) under "Guillem": "It breeds yearly on the steep Cliffs ... Likewise on an Island or Rock called *Godreve*, not far from St. *Ives* in *Cornwal*".

"Mur(re)" generally applied to the Razorbill in Cornwall, as noted in Ray (1678, p. 323). "Foolish" indicated the bird's tolerance when approached closely. See also the next entry.]

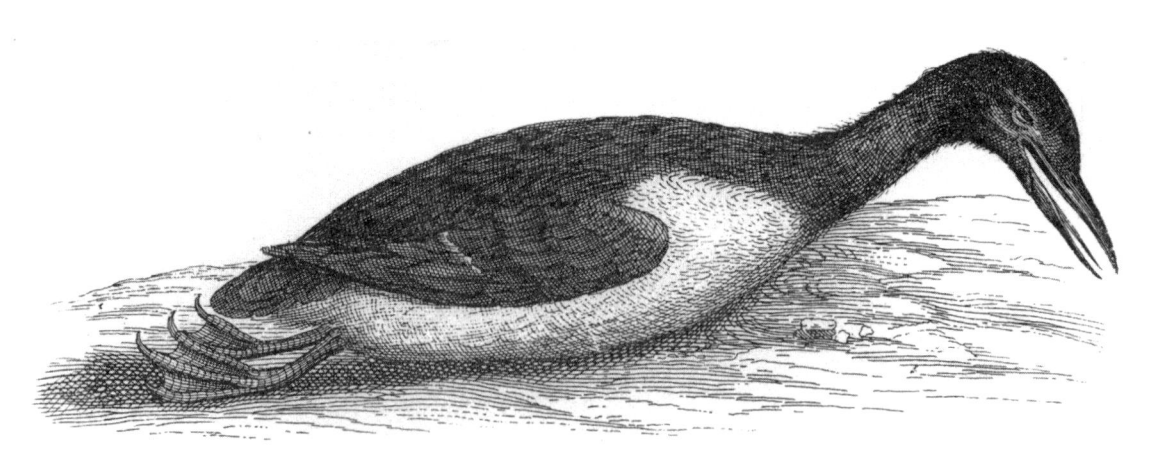

Guillemot, after Ray

168 Lesser Guillemot [Common Guillemot *Uria aalge*]

Although he states that it has the bill short, Fleming [1828, *History of British Animals*] speaks with confidence of its being the Young of the Foolish Guillemot: a circumstance scarcely credible, when we consider that it seems to be a law of Nature that the bills of birds are as large at their birth as in their after life. Another presumptive proof is that the Lesser Guillemot is a winter visitant.

[Couch soon realised his error and the Lesser Guillemot does not appear in his 1838 published account where Foolish Guillemot is correctly described as the Common Guillemot.

In his early notes, Couch refers only to Murs which could be either Guillemot or Razorbill (i, 27; ii, 19, 58; iii, 45, 150). In November 1819 he "Observed a Mur diving - the longest time I saw it remain under water was 50 seconds - between each dive if left to itself, it usually continues above as long as it continued below, before it dives again" (iii, 45). Both species can dive for this length of time.

Clement Jackson showed Couch a specimen of *Uria lacrymans* in mid-February 1843, "taken near Looe; & he thinks it is as common as the other" (viii, 296; *RRIC*, 1843, p. 29). At this time, the Ringed or Bridled Guillemot was thought to be a distinct species, but it soon became apparent that it was only a variety of the Common Guillemot. It is rarely found breeding on cliffs in the south of Britain, its numbers increasing northwards to around 20 per cent in Shetland.]

169 Spotted Guillemot [Black Guillemot *Cepphus grylle*]

A Specimen was shot in Falmouth in 1822: the back was blotch'd dusky white, the lower parts white. [Added later] A specimen taken at Looe Octr, 1831 [*J*, v, 167], the size of a Puffin, inside of the mouth and legs, bright red, bill dark; head grey;

back dark speckled; wings dark; the scapulars white; white below - a white body more or less speckled; answering to Fleming's description of C. grylle in winter clothing.

[This accurately described the winter plumge of this uncommon visitor to Cornish waters. The only previous record is of "one shot and cased" by Walter Moyle of Bake, St Germans, in 1718.]

170 [Added later] Red throated Diver [Red-throated Diver *Gavia stellata*]
The first Speckled Diver of Bewick.

[This is the immature and non-breeding plumage noted above under "Speckled Diver". On 31 March 1849, Couch records one "Shot at Pont & brought to me" (ix, 161). Pont refers to Pont Pill, a creek on the east side of the Fowey estuary at Polruan.]

Puffins

171 Razor Bill [Razorbill *Alca torda*]
Common on the Coast in Summer. Two Razor Bills & 3 Blackbill'd Auks were shot, April 3rd, at Looe. The former in Summer, the latter in Winter plumage. [Added later] Yet they are the same Species.

[See also the next entry.]

172 Blackbill'd Auk [Razorbill *Alca torda*]
Common on the Coast in Winter. The throats of the Auks above mentioned were perfectly white, & one had the full siz'd & mark'd bill. This decides the difference of these two Species.

Razorbill (left: summer plumage) and "Black-billed Auk" (winter plumage), after Bewick

[Couch initially followed Bewick in assuming two species were involved, but after examining one in 1832 (vi, 8), he realised they were one and the same: "a Specimen taken Feby 18 was in moult: new feathers were coming out, easily discernible on moving up the old ones: the white throat was changing to black: the sooty feathers were found displacing the black ones on the upper parts of the body: line from bill to eye still rather dusky". In 1830, three were killed with two Razorbills at Looe on 3 April, "the former in their winter & the latter in the Summer plumage" (v, 122).]

173 Puffin [Atlantic Puffin *Fratercula arctica*]
A summer visitant.

[It is unfortunate that Couch says nothing more of a species that probably nested in his day on some south coast islands. Puffin's eggs are reported to have been found on Gull Rock, Veryan, as recently as June 1951. In 1968 a Portloe fisherman told me that "a few had bred there up to about ten years or so ago" and that he remembered "large flocks of the 'sea parrots' about the rock in the 1920s". It is doubtful if more than about a dozen pairs of this once numerous breeding bird now nest on islands off the north Cornish coast. Annet remains the main breeding colony on Scilly.]

174 Little Auk [*Alle alle*]
Scarce. Mr Jackson has seen two specimens kill'd in Falmouth harbour, & one shot in Swanpool.

[These are amongst the earliest Cornish records of a species sometimes found well inland after violent gales. The first to be published dates from 1823 when Henry Mewburn sent to Thomas Bewick a bird caught in a brook on 5 October at Treskelly, St Germans, a mile and a half inland (Fox, 1827, p. 254). Another was taken at Looe on 28 October 1844: "This is our real Mur, the name being derived from the Sound it utters. I do not believe it uncommon on our Coast, but it is not often taken" (ix, 2). Local fishermen obtained another on 10 November 1860 (x, 500). Couch's last bird entry (xii, 207) on 18 January 1870 is for a Little Auk taken to him and from which he sketched the head with "no white spot over the eye. Young bird of the Year." The small white patch at the upper margin of the eye is a feature that is present, but only very small, in juvenile birds.

"Mur", "morr", or more commonly "murre" is local dialect, perhaps connected to Cornish *mor* (sea), as in *morvran* ("sea-crow") Cormorant. Murre has become general in North America for the guillemots, but not for the Little Auk which is there called Dovekie.]

Shag kind

175 Cormorant [Great Cormorant *Phalacrocorax carbo*]
Common. We have also the Crested Cormorant (P. Cristatus) which Montagu seems to have proved to be no more than a variety of the Common Cormorant.

[Crested Cormorant was sometimes applied to this species in summer plumage, but more usually and more appropriately to the Shag which sports a distinctive crest in summer. *Pelecanus cristatus* was first used by Pennant for the Shag which he called a Shag Cormorant. Couch was well aware of the differences between the two species: "The white spot on the thigh easily distinguishes this {Cormorant}, even when flying from the Shag, and is thus distinguished by the fishermen as having a watch under his wing" (*MNH*, 1830, p. 177).

In 1816, Couch wrote: "Be it remembered that the Bird which in the list of Birds I have call'd the Loom, as being so named with us, is the Cormorant Pelicanus Carbo" (ii, 41-42). "Loom", a variant of Loon, was widely used in Britain for various grebes and divers, and remains in common use in North America for the divers.]

176 Shag [European Shag *Phalacrocorax aristotelis*]
Common. Both this & the last Species become of a plain Colour in the winter.

Shag, after Yarrell

[William Yarrell noted in his *British Birds* (completed in May 1843) that one had been "caught in a crab-pot fixed at twenty fathoms below the surface". This information he evidently obtained from Couch who wrote in about March 1843 (viii, 297) that "In a crabpot lately put to Sea a Shag was taken, in a depth of water of 20 fathoms, near Gorran. It had entered to reach a Starfish & other things found in the pot. From Mr Peach" (C.W. Peach, the coastguard and palaeontologist then living at Gorran.).

Couch's first note on this species in December 1815 (i, 81-82) deals with the Shag's flight and method of feeding; "by moving its wings very quick, & not like the Gull, by sailing. They seem to be very incapable of making head against strong wind. It is curious to see a Shag manage a flatfish when it has caught it. It rolls the fish into a cylinder, before it swallows it." In about November 1844 (ix, 7) he recorded the diving time of a Shag in the harbour at Polperro; "the longest time I noted it to remain under water was 40 seconds". Birds have been recorded submerged for up to 170 seconds, though the average is around 53.]

177 Gannet [Northern Gannet *Morus bassanus*]

A common Bird in its Season. It commonly arrives on the Coast about the middle of September; but I have known it taken on the 20th of June. Many have been seen so late as the middle of April, which seems to imply either that they do not go far from us to breed; or that some may omit to breed during the Year. It is a matter of surprise to our fishermen, that when Gannets are very numerous, & falling on a Scul [school] of fish, whilst many are on the water, and many below, that they do not kill one the other; but tho' they are as thick as they can huddle & are perpetually falling from a great height with excessive violence, & in a perpendicular direction, no accidents are known to occur [1829, *J*, v, 82]; - except indeed in one instance which I remember, when the spine of the dorsal fin of a Gurnard, pierc'd the eye of a Gannet that fell on it: but they never fall on each other.

Our fishermen inform me that it is not uncommon to see what they believe to be a Gannet, nearly all black above, & white below. One such is on our Coast at the beginning of May 1830, in Company with other Gannets [3 May, *J*, v, 122]. Pennant describes the Young Gannet as Dusky, speckled with triangular spots, in Colour bearing a resemblance to the Speckled Diver; but is it possible that a Young Bird could be on our Coast so early as May?

Gannet, adult and immature (behind), after Yarrell

[Indeed it is possible, as Couch confirmed on 8 June 1832 (vi, 24) and acknowledged in 1838, noting that adult and immature birds may be "seen with us in all the months of the year". Gannets then nested on Lundy, and did so in decreasing numbers until 1909 (Gannets' Rock and Gannets' Bay lie at the north-east end of the island). That fact together with the vast shoals of Pilchards that periodically invaded Cornish waters in the 19th century meant that Gannets were more numerous inshore more frequently than now. Fishermen watched them as a guide to the movement of Pilchard shoals just below the surface. Couch wrote on 21 October 1815 (i, 61-62): "I have this day seen Gannets falling on fish. They beat about the sea, sometimes high & at others near the surface, but they always plunge from a height, whilst flying along they suddenly fall, as if arrested by a ball in their course, & plung headlong perpendicularly, with wings half extended into the sea; the sea flies around, & they continue under water while one might with moderate haste count twenty". The seining period was commonly from September to Christmas but varied over the years. On 6 May 1829 (vii, 65-66) "Pilchards are now in considerable abundance at 3 leagues or more from land ... Gannets now abound, falling on these Pilchards".

Gannets are rarely seen flying over land, but on 9 April 1829 (v, 63-64), Richard Bunt reported "that Gannets are numerous now at 10 leagues from land. He was once witness to the following fact. He was at Colmans in Lansallos Parish when he saw a gannet flying over the brake on Langreek estate opposite. The Bird fell in the Brake in the same manner as it was accustom'd to fall at Sea: he & another went over & found it with its neck broken."]

178 Little Petrel [European Storm-petrel *Hydrobates pelagicus*]
Not uncommon. In November 1795 Some hundreds of these Birds were seen for several days flying about Looe River. Bond's Hist. of Looe, p131. Numerous near the rocks, Octr 26, 1831.

[Thomas Bond's *Topographical & Historical Sketches of the Boroughs of East & West Looe,* London, was published in 1823. Storm Petrels still nest on Scilly, especially on Annet, but not often seen being nocturnal visitors to their nesting burrows. In Couch's day they bred on small islands off Cornwall, though the only record from the south coast is of single eggs taken from two nests by Mr Gill, the Falmouth taxidermist, "in the crevices of Gull Rock" {Veryan} on 30 June 1864. He also captured the sitting birds (W. P. Cocks, *RCPS*, 1864, pp. 9-10). Storm Petrels are sometimes driven inshore by stormy weather, as one found dead in the garden of R. G. Lakes at Trevarrick, St Austell, in January 1839 (*WB*, 11 i).

Walter Moyle of Bake wrote a good description in a letter dated 19 September 1716: "... it is generally seen off at Sea, a good distance from the Land, is almost perpetually on the wing and rarely observ'd to alight anywhere, and scarce ever appears ashore. In misty Weather, it flies near the Fishermen's Boats, who sometimes knock it down with their Poles; and 'tis very difficult to take it any other time" (Sargeant, 1726). Their flight appears rather weak and fluttering. Local fishermen told Couch in June 1837 "that when this bird seizes any thing on the water that is too large for its mouth, it runs backward with it for two or three yards, or more - not forwards, nor does it lift & carry it off - of course the wings are spread still" (vii, 219). I can find no confirmation of this habit, though it is known that birds may be blown backwards (P. Harrison, 1983, *Seabirds*, p. 272). There is no doubt at all about the habits of a bird in Polperro harbour on a windy 27 October 1852: "It has a light active flight - somewhat like a Swallow ... It seems short sighted; for it flies along very near the surface - only an inch or two above - as if looking for anything close at hand. Sometimes for an instant it stops as if alighting, but only for an instant; it seems scarcely concious of an enemy, & two were caught by boys - I believe easily" (x, 93-4). Their indifference to humans is well known.]

In his *Cornish Fauna* (1838, p. 30), Couch noted that the petrel figured by Borlase (1758, Plate XXIX, see p. 20) was thought by Dr J. Fleming to be the Fork-tailed (Wilson's) Petrel "chiefly on account of the great length of its wings". However, the engraving is not good enough to be precise and Borlase's bird does not show the yellow patches on the webs of the feet so clearly shown in Yarrell's figure (see **243**).]

179 Shearwater [Manx Shearwater *Puffinus puffinus*,
Sooty Shearwater *P. griseus*, Great Shearwater *P. gravis*]

Not uncommon. A Specimen all over lead colour'd, above and below 1833 Oct: which proved to be the Fulmar: rather the Cinerous Shearwater, Eyton's Rarer Birds p49. The Fulmar must therefore be omitted. [Added later] Not so. [See below under Fulmar.]

Great Shearwater with Sooty Shearwater (behind), after Yarrell

[The Manx Shearwater is the most common of the genus, especially during the autumn migration. On 16 September 1835, Couch wrote: "These Birds abound at a short distance from land, & are so bold or ignorant as to watch for the fisherman's bait, which they seize as he throws it from his hand. Hence they are caught easily, suffering themselves to be taken with the hand" (vii, 19).

Local fishermen called it "skidden" (iii, 133), but it is doubtful if they generally distinguished one species from another. Captain Willimott shot at, but could not retrieve, a bird a few days before 17 September 1818, "standing on the ground near a rill of water, which he had no doubt was the Bird commonly known by the name of Man of War Bird, & by sailors called the Boatswain ... having often seen it between the Tropics" (ii, 143-4). Boatswain was a seaman's name for various species of shearwater (though more usually for Tropic Birds, *Phaeton* spp.) as was Man-of-war Bird for the Manx Shearwater. Another local name, one I have not seen elsewhere, is "lordy" used by Couch on 4 October 1816 in describing a bird caught by a boy at sea using a hook baited with fish. The bird was unquestionably a Manx. The fishermen said that these birds pursue gulls and "make them drop their excerement, & then devour it; in the same manner as the Tom Horrey {skua} does" (ii, 52-3). For "excrement" read regurgitated food; even so, this is wrong, the fishermen mistaking skuas in company with the shearwaters. There does not appear to be any evidence that shearwaters harry other seabirds; all their food, mostly fish, they obtain by seizing it from the surface, or when pattering over the surface in the manner of storm-petrels, and by shallow diving.

The Cinerous Shearwater is the rarer Sooty Shearwater, but large numbers, sometimes thousands, are occasionally reported in the autumn migration. Two specimens figured by Yarrell (1843, Vol. III, p. 502) as the "Greater" Shearwater were supplied by D. W. Mitchell of Penzance, and illustrate the difficulties of identification at that period. As noted in the 4th edition of Yarrell (1884-5, Vol. IV, pp. 12-16), the shearwater with the pale underparts and dark cap is the Great Shearwater taken off Newlyn in November 1839 when large numbers were reported. The all-dark bird that Yarrell originally assumed to be its young is the Sooty Shearwater, also taken in Mount's Bay about the same season in 1838. Couch's "all over lead colour'd" bird must also have been the Sooty Shearwater, taken alive to Couch in October 1833 "having seized a fisherman's bait" (vi, 72).]

180 Fulmar [Northern Fulmar *Fulmarus glacialis*]

Exceedingly rare; but I suppose it to be the Bird which a fisherman describ'd, as coming about his Boat, having the figure & actions of a Petrel, but the size of a Blackbird, dark grey or bluish grey on the back, light below. It came so near, that he attempted to knock it down with a stick. [Added later in margin] I have obtain'd a Specimen of the Fulmar: & believe have ascertain'd the Bird here alluded to, to be the Grey Petrel Pr. cinerea: I saw a Specimen in the British Museum. This must be distinguish'd from Puffinus Cinereus [Sooty Shearwater], Eyton p49, which is a far larger Bird.

[The size of the Fulmar is underestimated. It was seen by Jonathan Marks about the end of October 1829 (v, 96; vii, 9). "Grey Petrel" was not a current English name for this species and may have been Couch's translation of the British Museum's label if it used the old scientific name *Procellaria cinerea* employed by M-J. Brisson in his *Ornithologie* (Paris, 1760). About late September 1833, he described another "caught with an hook ... that was lead colour'd all over, a little darker on the back & head, lighter below, but in no place darker than what is call'd dove colour" (vi, 32). Couch visited the British Museum when staying with William Yarrell in August 1835 (vii, 9). The Fulmar, formerly a northern species, was very rare on the Cornish coast throughout the 19th century, only becoming more common in the 1930s with breeding first proven in 1944 at Marble Cliffs, Trevone.]

181 Forktail'd Petrel [Leach's Storm-petrel *Oceanodroma leucorhoa*] Figure in Bewick's Br. B. Vol2, last Ed. [1826] - rare, but several Specimens.

Leach's Storm-petrel, after Bewick

[In 1838, Couch wrote, "I have known the taking of several Specimens, in stormy weather, late in the year". In December 1835 "a flock has been on our Coast for about a week; One flew into a Smith's shop at Seaton, another was found dying, floating on the surface of the Sea; & three others were shot" (vii, 47). This conforms with modern records, most of which are for October and November with large "wrecks" after particularly stormy conditions. Couch first received and fully described a specimen on 13 December 1831, "found dead this morning, at Penellick [Pennellick] near Pelynt; kill'd I suppose by last night's Storm. This is the first that has been recognis'd in Cornwall" (vi, 2). On 21 December he noted that Clement Jackson had received another from Truro, and that three or four were seen at Looe "within these few days. Both those taken were males" (vi, 2-3).]

Terns

182 Common Tern [*Sterna hirundo*]

It visits us in September, & sometimes remains until November.

[In Couch's day it may have bred sparingly on parts of the Cornish coast, as well as on Scilly where it still does, but the only published Cornish record is for July 1864 when Henry Bullmore jun. is said to have taken eggs from a nest at Newlyn "on the sand, and protected by loose stones" (W. P. Cocks, *RCPS*, 1864, pp. 9-10).

No mention is made of the similar Arctic Tern *Sterna paradisaea* in Couch's early accounts, although the species had been separated by Temminck in 1820. Couch initially followed Fleming (1828) who regarded the Arctic as a variety of the Common Tern. However, in May 1842 he wrote of "multitudes along our shores & harbours, of six shot by Mr Jackson, 5 were males; the female without enlarg'd eggs" (viii, 263), and on 6 October 1846 "several young Arctic & one old St. Hirundo" (ix, 99). The Arctic Tern nested on Scilly where E. H. Rodd reported that "they breed annually" and in greater numbers than the Common Tern (*Pz*, 1850, p. 430). By the early 20th century the Arctic was in the minority (J. Clark, 1902, *JRIC*, p. 222-3).]

183 Lesser Tern [Little Tern *Sterna albifrons*]

It visits us with the Common Tern.

[The species may have nested regularly on isolated shingle beaches in Cornwall, though published records are rare. James Clark was glad to announce in May 1905 that "the Lesser Tern ... still breeds in the county. Long may the locality continue to escape observation!" (*JRIC*, 1906, p. 355). The Little Tern may well have been the species Couch reported in 1832: "July 14. Several Terns, of rather small size, have been seen by our fishermen in the early part of the month. All Terns are call'd by them Mirets" (vi, 25), a dialect name confined to Cornwall and of unknown etymology.]

184 Sandwich Tern [*Sterna sandvicensis*]

Mr C. Jackson shot a specimen out of a flock, at Looe, towards the end of March 1828; which is the only time he has seen them.

[This is the earliest of the terns on spring migration, and a regular visitor. It is strange that the Polperro fishermen did not distinguish this larger species with its distinctive call. It nested on Scilly with over 100 nests reported in 1841 (Clark & Rodd, 1906, p. 31). But numbers declined and largely disappeared from its favoured nesting ground on Annet in the mid-1880s with no nests found after 1905 (Clark, 1908, *JRIC*, p. 282) until 1978.]

185 Roseate Tern [*Sterna dougallii*]

Roseate Tern, probably from Scilly, after Blight

[Couch made no comment. His first reference to this species in 1830 (v, 128) was copied from the newspaper (*RCG*, 29 v): "A number of those beautiful & scarce Birds the Roseate Tern, were shot at the Scilly Islands in the beginning of the Week. Some of them are now in the possession of Mr T. P. Dixon, Bookseller, Falmouth, for the purpose of preserving them." They nested on Scilly and were "tolerably common" when D. W. Mitchell went there in May 1840 (Clark & Rodd, 1906, p.32). Mitchell sent one together with a Sandwich Tern and a Curlew Sandpiper to Clement Jackson who told Couch so on 26 January 1842 (viii, 240). On a visit to Penzance in 1844, Couch noted "20 at once in the hands of the bird Stuffer" (viii, 337). Almost certainly the "stuffer" was W.H. Vingoe, and one of his specimens that J.T. Blight figured (1861, p. 90). All Blight's bird drawings were from specimens set up by Vingoe, most of which passed into Rodd's collection. Roseate Terns have rarely bred on Scilly in recent years.]

Gulls

186 Great black back'd Gull [Great Black-backed Gull *Larus marinus*]
It is call'd with us the Strip. I have known two or three pairs in our neighbourhood; but they seem to be of a wandering disposition, & do not remain long in a place.
[This is a more common breeding gull now, though most plentiful on the north coast and in the far west of Cornwall. Couch added it to his list of birds on 25 May 1816 (ii, 16) as "no common species with us ... of which the description in Gregory's Cyclopaedia [Gregory, 1813] applies correctly with the addition, that at the extremity of the lower chaps, there appears thro' the Spy-glass to be a red mark". This not only shows his accurate observation, but is also one of the rare occasions when he

mentions using a telescope which he must have done frequently. Also in May 1816 (ii, 18), Couch noted that three or four pairs were "breeding at different places along the coast, but not near each other; & that they will fight Ravens boldly". On 11 December the same year (ii, 65), he satisfied himself that it "continues with us all the Year".

"Strip" or "stripe" seems to have been a name peculiar to the local fishermen and alluded to the long black wings (ii, 65).]

187 Lesser black back'd Gull [Lesser Black-backed Gull *Larus fuscus*]

[No information given, nor in Couch's published 1838 account. There is no proof that it nested on the south coast of Cornwall east of the Lizard peninsula. Couch may have confused this summer migrant with other species (see Herring Gull below).]

188 Herring Gull [*Larus argentatus*]

Common.

[In common with other early naturalists, Couch found difficulty in separating species of gulls. In his first note in 1815 he wrote: "There are two species of gulls which are common on our coasts, the grey Gull & a brown gull. Their manners appear to be very similar" (i, 78). These are clearly adult and juvenile respectively of the Herring Gull, the most widespread and abundant nesting gull on the coast. All his "grey gulls" are Herring Gulls, as in his 1820 story: "when the young ones are in their nests, & a person attempts to get to them, the old ones make a great outcry, & when the plunderer has reach'd the place he usually finds all the nests empty - the young ones, even those very young, have got into the crevices of the rocks out of sight" (iii, 53). Even his account in "this severe winter" (1820) must refer to the Herring Gull or possibly a black-backed: "the common Gulls - either L. canus or the brown Gull, have been seen to devour larks, as I am told - a Skylark has been taken from the stomach of a Gull by a fisherman here" (iii, 53). The main diet of the Common or Mew Gull is terrestrial and aquatic invertebrates and birds will often congregate in fields with Starlings to find them. On 17 June 1816 he wrote: "I observe the common grey gull to pursue & drive away the black back'd gull; the latter weaving to avoid a contest", as the Herring Gull would certainly do in the nesting season (ii, 21).

Couch also swapped around the scientific names for the Herring Gull and the Lesser Black-backed Gull, but corrected the error in his 1838 account. The mistake had been made by Montagu (1802). The Lesser Black-backed was first identified as a British breeding bird by Thomas Pennant who doubted whether it differed specifically from the Great Black-backed Gull rather than from the Herring Gull to which it is most closely related.

Lesser Black-backed Gull, after Bewick

Herring Gull, after Bewick

Common (Mew) Gull, after Bewick

Couch carefully examined specimens of Herring Gulls in March 1837 when he described two of slightly larger size and weight that had been killed by Clement Jackson. He wrongly concluded that they were a new species to which he gave the name Jackson's Gull in honour of his taxidermist friend (vii, 176).

Frequent references are made to gulls in general, as in mid-October 1868 when Porbeagles, in pursuit of small fish, were leaping clear of the water. "Gulls were also on the watch, to seize the little fish driven on the surface by the Porbeagles" (xii, 137). Couch even took an interest in old wives' tales in his early years. In January 1816, after "confirming" that rain falls within 48 hours of a cat washing behind its ears, he contined: "when the gull flies at a great height, as if among the clouds, it portends wet & windy weather. But this latter is not so certain a sign as the former" (i, 97).]

189 Grey Gull [Mew Gull *Larus canus*]

Common.

[The Mew Gull, until recently invariably known as the Common Gull, is a passage migrant and winter visitor to Cornwall and often congregate in fields miles inland as well as frequenting estuaries. It does not nest in the south-west peninsula. Couch confused it with other similar species and there is no proof that Couch was familar with the Mew Gull (see under Herring Gull above).]

190 Little Gull [*Larus minutus*]

Bewick was under a mistake in reference to this Species, when he figur'd the Young of the Kittiwake in its place; as he seems indeed, to admit in a letter to me. The Specimen from which my Sketch was taken, is in the possession of Mr Clement Jackson, at East Looe. It was shot at Falmouth; weighed 4 ounces, & was very fat. I have heard of another shot on the Tamar. [Added later] Eyton (Rarer Birds) p 61, represents Mr Jackson's Specimen as a young Bird.

[Couch headed his account with a drawing (opposite) of a supposed young Little Gull shot in Falmouth harbour by Clement Jackson in October 1824 (*J*, v, 74; *MNH*, 1830, p. 177). However, the patern of light and shade around the head, the dark back and deeply forked tail indicate a young Sabine's Gull (*L. sabini*) and I am grateful to Tim Melling of the British Ornithologists' Union for drawing my attention to this. If accepted as authentic, it is the first Sabine's Gull in Britain, though an earlier one occurred in Ireland (see **265**).

Little Gull, after Eyton: not, as Couch supposed,
an immature which has a black tail band across the end

Couch's supposed Little Gull, actually an immature Sabine's Gull

The Tamar Little Gull was shot twenty miles up river by J. Whipple, a Plymouth surgeon, on 28 September 1828, and an immature was also shot on the Tamar in October 1831 (D'Urban & Mathew, 1892, p. 385). In Bewick's *British Birds* (1826), the illustration referred to by Couch appears under "The Young Kittiwake", the Little Gull having no illustration. The young of both species are somewhat similar. Little Gulls were reported by D. W. Mitchell (*MNH*, 1839, p. 467): an immature male in moult from St Ives Bay, 26 December 1838, its "central tail feathers one inch shorter than the outermost" suggesting a mis-identified Sabine's Gull, but the description is inadequate; and an adult shot in Penzanze harbour on 4 March 1839, apparently accompanied by another which escaped.

In January 1869, Couch saw at Stephen Clogg's house one shot "last week" out of a party of twelve at Looe, while on 10 February he noted that "very many" had been seen lately "on our Coast, & many starved to death on the shore - one found in our street, in consequence of the long continued stormy weather and boistrous Sea that seems to prevent their obtaining subsistence" (xii, 144, 148).]

191 Blackheaded Gull [Black-headed Gull *Larus ridibundus*]
Common in winter, at which time the black on the head disappears & is replaced by white, except a dark spot behind the Ear.

[In January 1820 (iii,52-53), Couch described in detail under the name *Larus Cinerarius* a specimen he had dissected, his interest stemming from the fact that Bewick had wrongly assumed two species were involved, the bird in winter plumage being called the Red-legged Gull. Identification continued to cause problems. In his account of birds washed in dead in the hard winter of 1829-30 (viii, 76), Couch included the Kittiwake, adding at the end of the paragraph "The Kittiwake here mentioned is the Blackheaded Gull". Not until William Yarrell published volume III of his *British Birds* (1843) did identification become somewhat easier.

A widespread name for the Black-headed Gull was Laughing Gull, a translation of its current Latin name. Couch used it in 1853 (x, 163) when he visited the Royal Cornwall Polytechnic Society in September and saw one in the Hall "killed this month". Laughing Gull now applies to an American species (*Larus atricilla*), also black-headed, not noted in Britain until seen near Eastbourne, Sussex, on 2 July 1923. The fourth for Britain was seen on St Agnes, Scilly, on 31 October 1967.

Particularly interesting are observations of a bird in December 1822, described "as best he could with a glass". It was the size of the "Red-legged", but "a band of white circles the forepart of the wings & includes all the quill feathers to the tip, no black point to the wings and tail - it seem'd to fly with a more active & irregular flight than the common gull {Herring Gull}, more minute particulars I could not see" (iii, 152). The following January there were two, except that "one of them has a narrow dark stripe across the wings" (iii, 154). Couch had no idea what these were, suggesting either immature Great Black-backed or "*L. canus*" by which he probably meant Herring Gull rather than the

Mew (Common) Gull. In October 1823 there were three of these birds "about the size of a pigeon", again commenting on the all-white quill feathers. "They are much smaller than the L. canus; but if last Year's birds were the young they would now have attain'd the full size. For this reason I rather incline to believe them a distinct species; the only one they are similar to is the L. Islandicus {Iceland Gull}, tho' the latter is, I believe, a larger bird." Later he inserted here "They are Larus Tridactylus, the Kittiwake" (iv 1-3). Kittiwakes they could not have been, except the one with the dark stripe across the wings. The size and plumage of the others best fit the adult Mediterranean Gull (*L. melanocephalus*), a species so closely related to the Black-headed Gull that they can interbreed. Unfortunately, the description is inadequate for the records to be accepted as Britain's first Mediterranean Gulls.

The Mediterranean Gull is now regularly reported on the Cornish coast. It has bred in Hampshire since 1968 and elsewhere more recently, though not yet in the south-west. The species was not officially regarded as British until one was shot near Barking on the Thames in January 1866, although two in a collection from Hawkstone, Shropshire, "now in possession of Mr Beville Stanier of Peplow Hall, Shropshire" were killed near Falmouth in March 1851 (*British Birds*, 1907-8, p. 328; Z, 1907). Hawkstone was the home of Rowland Hill (1795-1879), inventor of the postage stamp, who had a large bird collection, including the extinct Great Auk. His collection was sold after his death to Beville Stanier (E. Fuller, 1999, *The Great Auk*, p. 221).]

192 Kittiwake [Black-legged Kittiwake *Rissa tridactyla*]

In winter. A specimen of the Tarrock or young Kittiwake was shot at Looe Aug. 13, 1829.

[Tarrock, still used by birdwatchers for the young Kittiwake, was originally believed to be a separate species. The name also seems to have been used for the Black-headed Gull in Cornwall, at least at Mousehole into the 1920s (R. M. Nance, *A Glossary of Cornish Sea-words*, published posthumously in 1963).

Identification of this species proved very troublesome to Couch, understandably so considering the error in Bewick's *British Birds* noted above under Fulmar. Illustrations of confusingly similar gulls were quite inadequate. Couch reported seeing a Kittiwake on 2 December 1825: "I have thus repeated proof that this Bird comes here only in Winter, for I have never seen one of them during the Summer" (iv, 124). It is the most pelagic of the gulls, rarely seen outside the breeding season close inshore except in stormy weather. Bullmore (1866) called it "common in winter", but said nothing about breeding birds.

Kittiwakes now nest in colonies on the north Cornish coast and on the south coast mostly west of the Lizard, but little is known of their status in the 19th century when breeding may have been largely confined to the Isles of Scilly. Dialect "Annet" for the Kittiwake has nothing to do with Scilly, the name coming from Yorkshire. Birds breeding in large numbers on Men-a-vaur in 1852 are mentioned in a letter, but the site was vacated for Gorregan in the Western Rocks, only to diminish from the '70s with only one nest found in 1900 (Clark & Rodd, *Z*, 1906, p. 33). Colonies existed in west Cornwall by the end of the century, Clark noting them at Mullion Island, at Gull Rock off Veryan, "and occasionally at least on the mainland" (*JRIC*, 1902, p. 225). The British breeding population greatly increased during the 20th century.

Kittiwake (immature), after Bewick

In Couch's day, it is likely that the main south-western breeding colonies were those on Scilly and on Lundy island off north Devon. Indeed, it was the slaughter of young Kittiwakes on Lundy, and even larger numbers at Flamborough Head, Yorkshire, to satisfy the craze for ladies' hat plumes, that prompted Alfred Newton to condemn the practise at a meeting of the British Association for the Advancement of Science in 1868. The result was the 1869 Sea Birds Protection Bill referred to by R. Q. Couch in my Introduction. Howard Saunders, who edited the account of the Kittiwake in the 4th edition of Yarrell's *British Birds* (Vol. III, p. 653), witnessed the destruction on Lundy that continued for a fortnight or so from 1 August, the day the Protection Bill expired for the season. "In many cases the wings were torn from the wounded birds before they were dead." Old and young were shot at, "the mangled victims being tossed back into the water ... On one day 700 birds were sent back to Clovelly, on another 500, and so on" while "at least 9,000 birds were destroyed during the fortnight". Contemporary fashion writers were not all in favour of the slaughter of birds of one sort or another. "Flora R.", in *The Queen* (4 December 1875) felt "perfectly certain that no Englishwoman would wear a bird's wing or feathers, if she were aware how the bird had been killed with no other object than to supply the requirements of fashion" (Miles Lambert, 1991, *Fashion in Photographs 1860-1880*, p. 132). Happily, there is no evidence for such destruction in Cornwall, although it continued elsewhere thoughout the 1880s.]

193 Blacktoed Gull [Arctic Skua *Stercorarius parasiticus*. Long-tailed Skua *S. longicaudus*]

It is common in the offing while the Pilchard fishery lasts; but rarely comes very near the Shore. It is call'd Tomorry. [Added later] It is the Arctic Jager, Eyton's Rarer Birds p55, a good figure.

Long-tailed Skua, after Eyton (his Arctic Jager)

[The dialect name is usually written as Tom Horry or Tom Harry. It is derived from OE *horig* (filthy) or, perhaps more likely, Anglo-Saxon *hergian* (lay waste) in deference to the birds habit of harrassing other sea birds in order to pinch their food. I heard the name used by a Portloe fisherman as recently as 1968.

Confusion reigned over the distinction between the different species of skuas. In August 1816, Couch described a bird he could not then identify, adding later in pencil "wagel", Cornish dialect for the Arctic Skua: "The little brown Gull, not described in Gregory's Cyclopaedia [Gregory, 1813], is brown all over, but the back, & upper parts of the wings are of a deeper brown; & the feathers of those parts are each edg'd with a rim of lighter brown; the tail is tipped with somewhat a deeper brown, & the bill is black" (ii, 29). The description more or less fits the variable plumage of a juvenile Arctic Skua. In 1838, Couch listed both Richardson's Skua and Arctic Jager. The former is the Arctic Skua and the latter the Long-tailed Skua. E. H. Rodd discussed the confusion and minutely described an Arctic Skua "which was killed in a disabled state by a dog, in a field in the parish of St Buryan, in 1835 (*RRIC*, 1838, p. 40-1).

On 9 June 1821 (iii, 110), Couch described a light phase bird taken at sea, noting that the two central tail feathers were twice as long as the others, a description that fits the Long-tailed Skua *S. longicaudus*, or Buffon's Skua as it was then called. This is the earliest British record of the Long-tailed Skua. Both the Arctic and Long-tailed Skuas had been given the specific name *parasiticus* by different authors.]

194 Skua Gull [Great Skua *Catharacta skua*]

Common in winter on the Coast: the difference in the Bill is the only distinction between the young of this Bird & that of the Black toed Gull [Arctic Skua]: the Colour is alike in both; brown all over, a little lighter in some parts; the feathers margin'd with light. Both Species take food from the Sea when unable to rob others.

[The Great Skua is a bulkier bird than the Arctic, and more gull-like in shape with a blunt tail. In 1838, Couch described it as "not uncommon in Autumn, at a few leagues from land, but never approaches the shore. I have obtained it from fishermen, who have caught it alive, with a baited hook". This was late in 1831 when one that "fought boldly" was taken with two immature Arctic Skuas on a line baited with fish liver. It weighed 3 lb 1 oz, its length 2 feet and wingspan 4 feet (v, 163). Thomas Holten saw a "Tom Horry ... catch & devour a Stormy Petrel" in about October 1833 (vi, 73). Couch assumed the predator was an Arctic Skua, but it is more likely to have been a Great Skua.]

Goosanders

195 The Goosander [Goosander *Mergus merganser*]

In Winter. A Specimen I examin'd had a less crest and smaller bill than that figur'd by Bewick.

[This specimen was amongst birds sent to Clement Jackson from west Cornwall in 1831 (v, 117). See also the next entry.]

Goosander, after Bewick

196 Dundiver [Goosander *Mergus merganser*, or Red-breasted Merganser *M. serrator*]

It will be seen from Fleming [1828] that it is still contested whether this is or not the female Goosander.

[Dun Diver was common dialect for female and immature birds of both species. Couch used the scientific name *Mergus castor*, Goosander, but he may not have appreciated the difference between it and the female Red-breasted Merganser. Male birds are distinct enough.]

197 Redbreasted Goosander [Red-breasted Merganser *Mergus serrator*]

Rare, & in winter only, like others of this genus.

[Couch followed Fleming in calling it a Goosander. Other authors preferred the now established name of Merganser.]

198 Smew [*Mergellus albellus*]

These four Species were kill'd in Cornwall in the severe winter of 1829-30.

[Three species only were involved in 1829-30 and 1837-38, as Couch corrected in 1838. In the joint paper Couch published in 1830 (*MNH*, p. 177), the Smew is described as "rare only in severe winters", a status unchanged today. Clement Jackson had one before April 1829 (v, 64) and another taken to him in February 1838 (vii, 270).]

199 Wild Swan [Whooper Swan *Cygnus cygnus*, Tundra Swan *C. columbianus*]

A number of these Birds, scarcely less than fifty, visited us in the severe winter of 1829-30; & several were shot in different parts of the County. One kill'd at Par measur'd seven feet & 6 inches across the wings; the weight (I believe) 14 pounds. One which I saw, stuff'd for the Museum at Truro, was much smaller than the others. They flew high, close together & with a flapping motion; after a short distance they arrange themselves in a Column. One shot at Looe, brought eighteen others to it by its cries. In taste & appearance the flesh resembles lean beef. The figure on the opposite page is from one of those now shot, & in Mr Jackson's possession at Looe.

[In January 1830, Couch was informed by Stephen Clogg of "13 Wild Swans flying over his house at Trelawny Mill, during the frost. One has been shot near Truro, one at Blissland {Blisland}, one at Par shot on 27 December 1829 was measured by Couch, & one at Looe; of these two at least were kill'd before Mr C. saw the flock; so that they must have been numerous at first. Jackson said the taste was much like lean beef. They fly high, near together, & with a flapping motion; after a short distance they arrange themselves in a Column" (v, 103, 106, 108-9). The *West Briton* made much of the invasion: on 8 January it reported three from Blisland and several from Looe on the 3rd, one of which was sold for £1 to a gentleman who sent it to a friend in Launceston. On 1 January it noted a number in Mount's Bay, some of which were killed, while on the 29th it reported three killed the previous Friday (22 January) "on the moors near Camelford by a labourer who sold them for five shillings each". The edition of 16th February recorded a flock of 16 at Scilly, some of which met the usual fate.

The Truro Museum specimen no longer exists. When presented to the Museum it was described as a Whistling Swan shot at St Clement Creek (i.e. Tresillian River) by a party of gentlemen. The unfortunate bird received good publicity in the *West Briton*: "Yesterday {31 December 1829} a party of Gentlemen {named on 19 February as Messrs John, Gregory and Edwards} who were on a shooting excursion on the Truro river, observed a wild swan, at which they fired; the bird, which was wounded flew off, but being pursued it contrived to keep the whole party on the alert for nearly two hours before they succeeded in bringing it down, which they did at length, after having fired upwards of forty shots at it." Because Couch described the Truro bird as much smaller than the others, it was most probably Bewick's Swan, a third smaller than the Whooper.

The distinction between the two species was detailed by William Yarrell in a paper read in January 1830 and published that May: "On a new Species of Wild Swan, taken in England, and hitherto confounded with the Hooper", *Transactions of the Linnean Society* (Vol. XVI, p. 445-54). Apart from the Whooper being larger, the important anatomical difference was in the trachea (windpipe). In both species the trachea enters a cavity formed within the keel of the breast bone, loops back out and then curves forward over the top of the breast bone where it divides in two and joins the lungs. Yarrell gave measurements of the most perfect specimens. In the Whooper, the loop was no more than 3 inches long within a breast bone exceeding 8 inches long; in Bewick's Swan the depth of insertion was 5 inches within a breast bone of nearly 6 inches, though in the youngest specimen he examined it posessed "only the vertical insertion of the fold of the trachea".

Couch read the paper and examined the tracheae of the bird sent to Truro Museum and of one "smaller than the others" preserved by Clement Jackson (v, 137-8). "In one the cavity is small & runs just half way back" (suggesting a Whooper); in the other, "a Young bird {it} runs 2/3 the way back & is double the size" (suggesting a Bewick's). Unfortunately, Couch's description is not full enough to be certain which trachea belonged to which specimen. Couch's sketch, with the long curving neck, suggests a Whooper, while the amount of pale colour (yellow) at the base of the bill is small enough to indicate Bewick's Swan, but bill patterns vary.

Couch's drawing of a Wild Swan

From a flock of six Wild Swans in Carrick Roads in January 1830, two were shot and one preserved by Mr N. Tresidder of Falmouth. From the description in Tresidder's note-book, Cocks was convinced it must have been the "*Cygnus Bewickii*" (*RCPS*, 1849, p. 46). It is sad that the name Bewick's Swan, given to this species by P. J. Selby and Yarrell in 1830 to honour "the memory of our late unrivalled engraver on wood", has now been swept into the dustbin of history and replaced with Tundra Swan.]

200 Cravat Goose [Canada Goose *Branta canadensis*]
Figure in Bewick's Br. Birds vol 2 p32 of the Supp. from a Specimen shot in Cornwall. Rare.

Canada Goose, after Bewick

[This is the bird illustrated by Bewick (1826 ed., p. 276) from the "perfect skin" of a specimen sent to Newcastle by Henry Mewburn of St Germans in 1821. It had been shot at Tredinnick, St Erney, by William Keast on 19 January 1819. A pair had also appeared on the lawn of Port Eliot, St Germans, on the 17th, one of which was shot, and Mewburn saw another shot by a miner on the moor near St Cleer (Fox, 1827, p. 141). These are the first records for Cornwall of a species introduced to Britain in the 17th century. The diarist John Evelyn apparently saw them in the collection of Charles II at St James's Park, London, on 9 February 1665 (Lever, 1977, pp. 259-60). Canada Geese have bred in Cornwall since 1983.]

201 Gray Lag Goose [Greylag Goose *Anser anser*]

Not common in its wild state.

[Domestic geese are descended from this species and give rise to feral birds that account for many records. Couch's only reference (x, 536) is to one shot at Marazion Marsh in early March 1862 (Rodd, 1864, p. 30). One was shot by Capt. Wallis near Restronguet Creek in the winter of 1848 (*RCPS*, 1857, p. 57).]

202 Whitefronted Goose [Greater White-fronted Goose *Anser albifrons*]

Large flocks of this Species were seen in the winter of 1829-30 [*J*, v, 108-9], frequenting turnip fields; & so many as five were in more than one instance kill'd at one shot. The flesh resembles that of an Hare.

[This is Couch's only note on this species. The White-fronted is still a scarce passage migrant and winter visitor to Cornwall, but from 1935 to 1973 a flock regularly wintered at the Walmsley Sanctuary created for them on the marshes of the River Amble, St Minver.]

203 Bean Goose [*Anser fabilis*]

[No information given by Couch, although he had seen one in February 1829 at Clement Jackson's house together with a Pochard and other wildfowl "killed in Cornwall" in the hard winter (v, 63). Edward Moore of Plymouth also reported "many" there in the hard weather of January 1830 (*TPI*, 1830, p. 342). There are few modern records, but according to E. H. Rodd (*Pz*, 1850, p. 424), it was the common wild goose "in severe winters in large flocks: unless there is a strong frost, and of some continuance, in the north, they are seldom seen in the southern and western counties". This was certainly the case in the winter of 1890-91 when flocks were seen throughout Cornwall and on Scilly (Clark, 1906).]

204 Brent Goose [*Branta bernicla*]

In a Specimen just then moulting, caught about 1st October [1829] the spot on the neck, as figur'd by Bewick, had only a few fragments of white, apparently in part from the loss of the feathers, the new ones not having protruded. Instead of the black terminating rather high in the neck by a definite line, it was spread over the breast, softening to a lighter, & mottled on the belly. Some old feathers remaining on the back & wings were brown, edg'd with ash; but the new feathers were black; so that when in full winter plumage the head, neck (except the white spot) breast, back & wings, would be uniformly of a sooty Colour.

Brent Goose, after Bewick

[Couch's specimen was shot "a day or two since among others, near Looe Island ... in the process of moulting" (v, 91-2). The white neck spot is absent in immature birds. The darkness of the breast indicates the dark-breasted subspecies of Siberian origin, the usual form seen in Cornwall as a scarce winter visitor that is not of annual occurrence. Geese can be difficult to identify at a distance in flight, so it is not surprising that Couch's first reference in 1815 (i, 75) is simply to a flock of "wild geese".]

205 Scoter [Black Scoter *Melanitta nigra*]

Common on the Coast in winter. A specimen was caught in Falmouth harbour Aug. 2, 1824.

[This was an immature bird in weak condition taken to Clement Jackson for preservation (v, 74). The Black or Common Scoter has been recorded off the Cornish coast in every month of the year, though mostly in small winter flocks.]

206 Surf Duck [Surf Scoter *Melanitta perspicillata*]

I quote this as Cornish, supposing it to be the Species described or figur'd, Loudon's Mag. Nat. Hist. Vol 2. [1829] p101 by the Rev. Mr Lakes.

[The Revd Lakes, boating with a friend early one morning in September 1826, noticed a dark bird at the mouth of a pill or creek in Fowey harbour. The friend shot it and Lakes sketched it at home, though before he could examine it more closely, a cat carried "it away to its own museum"! A copy of his sketch was published with the following description. "The bill, it will be observed, is remarkably large, and the forehead slopes more gradually to it than is usual in the case of the duck tribe. This bird is about the size of a wigeon, and, I should imagine, had not arrived to its perfect plumage, by the uncertain form of the white spots on the cheek." The nostrils were also noted as being "in the middle

Surf Scoter, Revd. Lakes' drawing

of the bill". The bird certainly resemles a female or immature Surf Scoter, as Couch saw from the illustrations of both sexes in Eyton (1826). The male is much more distinctive.

This American vagrant was already known from occasional examples, notably in Orkney and Shetland, but it has rarely been seen in Cornish waters. A decaying specimen, found "in a heterogeneous deposit" on a beach at Pendennis, Falmouth, after a violent winter gale in 1845, was graphically described by W. P. Cocks, the finder, as giving off "a powerful *noli-me-tangere* effluvia" (*RCPS*, 1857, p. 76).]

207 Wild Duck [Mallard *Anas platyrhynchos*]

Common in winter.

[Couch makes no other mention of this now common nesting bird. Although William Borlase (1758, p. 245) recorded it breeding "in the marsh betwixt Penzance and Marazion", it appears to have been a rare nester throughout the 19th century. Even E. H. Rodd (1880) only knew that "A few remain with us during the summer, and breed here and there in suitable localities". Couch's earliest note (i, 84) refers to "plenty" about Looe Island in December 1815.

The name Mallard (Old French *malart*) originally applied only to the male bird. Wild Duck was the more usual name until Mallard found favour in the 1912 *Hand-list of British Birds* by E. Hartert and others.]

208 Scaup Duck [Greater Scaup *Aythya marila*]

[No information given. "Scarce" in his published 1838 account applies equally today for this winter visitor. It had probably occurred in Cornwall in January 1829 when Drew, the Plymouth taxidermist, received specimens (*TPI*, 1830, p. 344), but the first dated Cornish specimen was an adult female shot in St Keverne parish on 19 January 1850 (*RCPS*, 1857, p. 77).]

209 Shield Duck [Common Shelduck *Tadorna tadorna*]

[No information given. Clement Jackson saw one at Looe in the winter of 1829-30 (v, 64). It was common only in hard winters, even though Richard Carew (1602) wrote that the "Burranet" nested in rabbit burrows. A few pairs nested in Devon in the 19th century (as at Braunton Burrows), but apparently in Cornwall only on the Camel estuary at the start of the 20th century (Clark, 1906). Shelducks declined in many parts of Britain in the 19th century, its subsequent increase in maritime counties "can be seen as a recovery under protection given both at home and in the Heligoland Bight" where many migrate to moult (J. T. R. Sharrock, Ed.,1976, *The Atlas of Breeding Birds in Britain and Ireland*, p. 94). Cornish and Scillonian breeding birds probably moult in Bridgwater Bay, Somerset.]

210 Shoveler [Northern Shoveler *Anas clypeata*]

Shoveler, after Bewick

Figure in Bewick's Br. Birds Vol2, p311; but in a Specimen shot in the winter of 1829-30, the bill was longer than is express'd in Bewick's figure.

[The bird was in the collection of Clement Jackson (v, 105) who had also shot one at Swanpool, Falmouth, in the winter of 1826 (*MNH*, 1830, p. 177). See also the next entry.]

211 Redbreasted Shoveler [Northern Shoveler *Anas clypeata*]

Montagu & Fleming pronouce it to be only a variety of the last Species.

[Montagu was the first to point out that these were the same species after examining a specimen of the "Red-breasted" shot on a pool in south Devon on 5 August 1807. It is the intermediate plumage of the male before it became fully adult when it was sometimes called the Blue-winged Shoveler.]

212 Wigeon [Eurasian Wigeon *Anas penelope*]

In winter.

[A Wigeon caught by some boys in January 1836 was kept by Couch in a cage until it died on 26 May. He made copious notes on its growth of new feathers and its restlessness at migration time (vii, 52-53, 59, 76). It is one of the most common estuary ducks in winter.]

213 Gadwall [*Anas strepera*]

Rare.

[The first Cornish specimen was killed in or before 1850 on Trengwainton ponds, Madron (Rodd, *Pz*, 1850, p. 425). Gadwall did not breed in Britain until about 1850 when a pair of migrants, caught in a decoy at Dersingham, Norfolk, were wing-clipped and released on Narford Lake in the Breckland. Birds were introduced to Tresco, Scilly, in 1934 and have bred there ever since. Wintering birds have gradually increased in Cornwall.]

214 Pochard [Common Pochard *Aythya ferina*]

Scarce.

["Scarce" could only have applied to Couch's neighbourhood. He saw one at Clement Jackson's, killed "in Cornwall" in the winter of 1828-9 (v, 63). Elsewhere it was always a regular winter visitor, though now more plentiful as a result of the construction of reservoirs. E. H. Rodd found it "not uncommon in the winter months after frost in the Land's-end district" (*Pz*, 1850, p. 426).]

215 Pintail Duck [Northern Pintail *Anas acuta*]

Scarce.

[Clement Jackson reported seeing one in the hard winter of 1829-30 (v, 109). It remains a rather scarce winter visitor and passage migrant, particularly to the Lynher and Camel estuaries.]

216 Goldeneye [Common Goldeneye *Bucephala clangula*]

Scarce. [See under the next entry.]

217 Morillon [Common Goldeneye *Bucephala clangula*]

Montagu entertains no doubt of this being identical with the Goldeneye.

[Morillon was a fowler's name for the female and immature birds formerly considered to be a distinct species. Clement Jackson reported seeing a "Morillon" in the hard winter of 1829-30 (v, 109). The species is now a regular passage migrant and winter visitor in small numbers to reservoirs and estuaries.]

218 Tufted Duck [*Aythya fuligula*]

[No data given and only "Scarce" printed in Couch's 1838 account. E. H. Rodd only found them in the Land's End district in winters "with more or less frost" (*Pz*, 1850, p. 427). Four shot at Penrice, St. Austell, and one taken in the Truro River in the winter were described as "very rare" (*WB*, 10 iii 1854). Tufted Ducks increased over much of northern Europe in the 20th century, including Cornwall where reservoir construction has favoured this freshwater duck. One or two pairs now breed in the County in some years. F. R. Rodd, in his annotated 1864 list of birds by E. H. Rodd, noted that a pair "bred wild" on Bodmin Moor in 1858 when Tufted Ducks were still regarded as "very rare in winter". Prior to this, F. R. Rodd kept some at Trebartha Hall, North Hill, where the unpinioned young left in the autumn but returned to breed in the following spring.]

219 Teal [Common Teal *Anas crecca*]

[Curiously for such a well known winter visitor, Couch makes no comment, but "most of the duck tribe" were scarce in south Cornwall (*MNH*, 1830, p. 177). E. H. Rodd called it the most regular of winter visitors to the Land's End district, "appearing sometimes early in the autumn, and at times in large numbers in the marsh pools" (*Pz*, 1850, p. 426). It has bred at reservoirs in Cornwall only rarely since about 1978.]

220 Spurwing'd Goose [Spur-winged Goose *Plectropterus gambensis*]

Spur-winged Goose, after Bewick

Figure in Bewick's Br. Birds Vol2, last Edition [1826]. The only Specimen known to have been taken in Britain, was caught at St Germans in June 1821.

[This species is not on the offical British list of birds. Even so, William Yarrell published it (1843), re-using Bewick's illustration back-to-front and modified in details of plumage and background. The bird has also been called the Ganser, Gambo, or Egyptian Goose. The last name also confuses it with the true Egyptian Goose (*Alopochen aegyptiacus*) which was introduced to St James's Park, London, and figured by Ray (1678).

The Spur-winged Goose must have escaped from captivity. It was first seen in fields adjoining the cliffs at Portwrinkle before being shot by John Brickford in a wheat field at Sconner on 19 June 1821. It was in perfect condition until his wife attempted to stuff it. She then cut off the wings for dusters and threw away the rest. About three weeks later, Henry Mewburn of St Germans sent a servant to recover the remains which were brought to him "covered with mud, the head torn off, but luckily preserved, as also one wing, when I had it washed, and put it together as well as I was able". The bird's head was recovered from a dunghill where it had been injured by the pigs, as Clement Jackson told Couch "on the authority of Mr Mewburn" (vi, 22). Mewburn sent it to Newcastle where Thomas Bewick drew it before it was "most ably re-set" by Richard Wingate, a Newcastle taxidermist (Fox, 1827, pp. 252-253).]

221 Black Swan [*Cygnus atratus*]

A Specimen of the Black Swan of New South Wales was sent to Mr Jackson, to be stuff'd, in January 1834; it having been kill'd in the west of Cornwall. It must have escaped from Captivity [*J*, vi, 77].

[This popular ornamental fowl was first imported into Britain in about 1791. It became well known with other exotica on the lake at Bicton, south Devon, but it is not known when they were introduced there. The ornamental lake with its two islands existed by 1812 (Todd Gray, 1995, *The Garden History of Devon*, University of Exeter), and Black Swans were recorded there in *The Gardener's Magazine*, 29 x 1842. A bird, almost certainly from Bicton, was captured near Exmouth at the end of October 1855 (*WB*, 2 xi). In its native habitat the Black Swan is a wanderer, rather than a true migrant, capable of flying for several hundred miles, though the origin of the Cornish specimen is not known. There are few references to the species in Britain, all the more curious considering that Bewick included such domestic birds as the Cock and Turkey. Couch omited it from his 1838 account. Nowadays, several are reported regularly, as are various other exotic escapees, rendering redundant the words of the Roman satyrist Juvenal:

Rara avis in terris nigroque simillima cycno.
(A rare bird on the earth and very like a black swan.)

Couch, himself no mean classical scholar, would doubtless have agreed in his declining years with another of Juvenal's maxims:

Tenet insanabile multos

Scribendi cacoethes et aegro in corde senescit.

(An inveterate and incurable passion for writing clings to many and grows old in their sick bodies.)]

SUPPLEMENT

IN this section are included those birds (other than domestic species) that Couch dealt with in *A Cornish Fauna* (1838) and its Appendices of 1841 (pp. 69-70) and 1844 (pp. 145-148), and in his MS "Journal of Natural History", that have not already appeared in the species' accounts in the main section of this book.

As Couch became increasingly immersed in marine studies, much of his bird information was gleaned from notes published by others. His *Journals* from 1862 to 1870 contain references to only nineteen species, whereas his index for 1844 to 1851 contains well over a hundred. Much of his later information came from notes published by E. H. Rodd (1810-1880), a solicitor by training who lived in Penzance, at 4 South Parade, from early in 1833 until his death. He was deeply involved in local affairs and, like Couch, concerned with the welfare of poor fishermen. He was a leading member of the Penzance Natural History and Antiquarian Society from its establishment in 1839 as one of its curators, and from 1862 to 1865 its Vice-President. Both he and Couch contributed notes to the Society's Annual Reports and those of the Royal Institution of Cornwall. Indeed, Rodd wrote the "Aves" section of the R.I.C.'s second edition of Couch's *Cornish Fauna* (1878), though it must be admitted this adds nothing of merit to the 1838 edition and is inferior to Rodd's other publications.

Rodd's portrait, published here for the first time, cannot have been taken much later than the early 1860s and shows him as a much younger man than appears as the Frontispiece to his *Birds of Cornwall* (1880) which contains a short Memoir of his life by James Edmund Harting. Rodd was well known throughout Cornwall and the early portrait is from the photographic album of Charles Lygon-Cocks of Treverbyn Vean, St. Neot.

Edward Hearle Rodd
(17 iii 1810 - 21 i 1880)

A Cornish Fauna, Part I, 1838, Royal Institution of Cornwall, Truro.

222 Blue Throated Warbler [Bluethroat *Luscinia svecica*]
A Bird supposed to be this species, as judged from its conspicuous colours at a small distance, was seen near Resprin [Respryn, Lanhydrock-St Winnow border], but not taken, towards the end of September 1836.
[The bird was seen at a distance of about 20 feet by William Minards, one of Couch's most reliable observers (vii, 122-123). It was described as "a Redbreast with a blue throat & a line of light colour encirling it: reddish behind the neck. The singularity of a bright blue breast in a bird struck him as remarkable ... The bird perch'd on a newly planted fir about 2 or 3 feet high, and when it saw him watching it, it flew among these trees & was lost to his sight." This is the first Cornish record of a scarce migrant usually recorded in September and October, notably on Scilly. The description is that of a male, but not good enough to say if it was the red-spotted or white-spotted form, though the white spot may be absent in the latter.

W. P. Cocks was shown the preserved skin of a Bluethroat before 1849, but doubted that it had been shot in the Falmouth district (*TN*, 1851, p. 40; Cock's Lithographed List, February 1849).]

223 Lesser Whitethroat [*Sylvia curruca*]
Rare.
[This is an uncommon migrant, mainly on Scilly in the autumn with fewer in spring; a pair nested there in 1965. It is doubtful if Couch had any reliable record. Col. George Montagu wrote in his MS "Diary" on 3 May 1797, "Believe I heard the Lesser Whitethroat", but evidently discounted it when he published his *Dictionary of British Birds* (1802), noting its absence from Devon and Cornwall. Courtney (1845, p. 27) wrote that it is "said to have occurred, if so, new to the county". W. P. Cocks reported that two were seen "in Mr Selley's second field leading to Budock Church," 14 March 1848 (*RCPS*, 1849, p. 41), an exceptional date if true, though not the earliest in Britain. The first authenticated Cornish specimen was an adult sent to E. H. Rodd from Scilly in October 1857 (*RRIC*, 1857, p. 19), but on the mainland not until 11 September 1902 when an immature was killed near Poundstock (Clark, 1907, p. 1).]

224 Whinchat [*Saxicola rubetra*]

Rare, not more than two or three Specimens having been recorded as Cornish.

[Couch may have based his statement on Montagu (1802) who wrote that it "is found rarely in the further part of Devonshire and in Cornwall". E. H. Rodd called it rare and local on the eastern moors, and occasionally (as a migrant?) on the open downs near Castle-an-Dinas, Ludgvan (*Pz*, 1850, p. 406). The position is little changed with scarce breeding confined to valleys on Bodmin Moor. It is a regular migrant in spring and autumn.]

225 Siskin [Eurasian Siskin *Carduelis spinus*]

Rare. A young Specimen was brought alive to me, October 31, 1835.

["It died shortly after being taken"(vii, 34). J. C. Bellamy (1839, p. 204) wrongly assumed that this young bird meant the species had nested in Cornwall. Siskins were scarce winter visitors to Cornwall up to the 1960s. Now they are more common with increasing breeding birds as a result of afforestation, especially around Bodmin Moor, with occasional proof of nesting as far west as Truro.]

226 Night Heron [Black-crowned Night Heron *Nycticorax nycticorax*]

Rare.

[Couch noted two occurrences in his *Journal*. The first (viii, 340) in 1844 at Penzance Museum, "taken at Redruth". This could be the male from Crowan parish reported "in the last three years" together with a female from the Lizard district and a juvenile caught between Penzance and Newlyn (*RRIC*, 1838, p. 39). The juvenile, Rodd originally described as a Gardenian Heron (an alternative early name) supposedly "in the nestling plumage" (hardly a credible description) taken alive to him. Couch, 1841, p. 69, quotes Rodd's account in full. Couch's second reference (ix, 224) must be the unfortunate bird "knocked on the head by David Smith in a clump of bushes on Tresco, Scilly, on 15 May 1849 (Clark & Rodd, 1906, p. 19).]

227 Garganey [*Anas querquedula*]

Scarce. It has been seen at the Swanpool [Falmouth] in April.

[The locality suggests a sighting by Clement Jackson, though none is mentioned in Couch's *Journal*. This migrant, often noted in early spring, has never been abundant. The *West Briton*, 13 iii 1840, reported that during the last week several had been shot near the Land's End "and have found their way into the cabinets of collectors". A male and female were also shot in the neighbourhood of Falmouth on 18 March 1852 (*WB*, 26 iii).]

228 Glaucous Gull [*Larus hyperboreus*]

Rare.

[There are few published early records. E. H. Rodd, who added to his collection one taken in Mount's Bay in early April 1872, stated in 1850 only that it was "occasionally observed, but by no means regularly" (*Pz*, 1850, p. 433). W. K. Bullmore saw two off Maenporth, Budock, in 1865 (*RCPS*, 1866, p. 44). Couch wrote in 1835 that "Mr Jackson has no doubt of his having possessed this Bird, taken at Falmouth; but at the time he had it he could not discover the name" (vii, 47-8).]

Appendix, 1841, based on Couch's account (with some alterations) presented to the Meeting of the British Association of Science at Plymouth.

229 Honey Buzzard [European Honey-buzzard *Pernis apivorus*]
A bird of the first year, killed in Cornwall, fell into the hands of Dr Leach, and is now in the British Museum.

This was the first Cornish specimen, now preserved in the national collection at Tring. It is a pale phase adult with a creamy-white head killed at Pencarrow, Egloshayle, in 1817 (Vellum Catalogue No. B16c; Peter Colson, *in lit*, 6, vi, 1975). The species is a regular but uncommon passage migrant. "Last week in June 1855 a Specimen ... caught at Carclew, Mylor, Cornwall Gazette" (x, 256). This was a young male in E. H. Rodd's collection killed about 28 June (*RCG*, 6 vii). A young female, also killed at Carclew, was presented to the R.I.C. between 6 November 1845 and 5 November 1846.]

230 Snowy Owl [*Nyctea scandiaca*]
Its occurrence in Cornwall is reported by Mr Bellamy, Nat. Hist. of south Devon, p. 200. The specimen is in the possession of the Reverend Mr Hore, where I had the opportunity of inspecting it. It had probably been driven hither by a storm, having suffered much from the weather.

[J. C. Bellamy (1839, p. 200) stated that it had been found at St Germans in December 1838 and "knocked down with a stick". It was actually caught at St John's Lake and taken by a boatman to Pincombe the Plymouth taxidermist. W. S. Hore, who was in his shop at the time, subsequently purchased it (D'Urban & Mathew, 1892, p. 134). The Revd Hore of Stoke Damerel had a fine collection of birds taken in the Plymouth region. Couch saw the bird in about early August 1841 (viii, 198).]

231 Woodchat Shrike [*Lanius senator*]
Reported by Mr Rodd of Penzance.

[An exhausted adult male was taken in a boat at Scilly in September 1840. Augustus Pechell also shot several immatures in autumn 1849, one of which was sent to E. H. Rodd on 5 October (*Pz*, 1849, pp. 290-91; J. Clark & F. R. Rodd, Z, 1906, p. 6). A young shrike that Couch sent Clement Jackson "long since - as found at sea", was identified by Jackson as a Woodchat Shrike, "as recognised by recent examination" (1855, x, 256).

On 1 June 1865, Couch was told of a bird supposedly breeding at "Roundfield above Palace Shooter", near Killigarth in Talland. He saw the bird at no great distance as he followed it along the road, but could see few distinguishing marks beyond the fact that it was brown, larger than a thrush, "nearly perhaps as large as the Grey Shrike - which I have seen", with a "tail of good length and wedge shaped" with white outer feathers. In flight "the tail became beautifully conspicuous ... the white border running so as almost to meet the white of the other side", as would be the case when looking at the underside of the tail. "I supposed I saw some other white on the body but could not be sure of it. I could not discern any part black - all seemed brown" (xi, 139-140). If the inadequate description correctly identifies the bird, it must have been a passage migrant, now expected annually in spring, especially on Scilly. Its distribution is mainly Mediterranean and it does not breed in Britain.]

232 Black Start [Black Redstart *Phoenicurus ochruros*]
Reported by Mr Rodd.

[This was a female shot near Penzance. Rodd gave no details in his 1840 paper (*RRIC*, p. 76), but must be the bird shot at Marazion Green according to J. S. Courtney (1845, p. 26). The species soon proved to be not uncommon and in his 1844 "Supplement" (p. 146), Couch described in detail what was evidently an immature shot by William Minards on 6 January 1842, after four days of frost, presumably in the Polperro area (*J*, viii, 237-8, 240), and knew of a male killed near Penzance in the same winter. In January 1845, William Minards was convinced he saw a male, presumably about Polperro, while C. W. Peach obtained "four Specimens at Gorran, at one time, this winter" (ix, 8-9,15). One was killed at "Killa" (Killigarth, Talland) in the first few days of November 1847, and "two others seen near the same place" (ix, 133-4). A female was shot and another "taken on pin & thread, bait a worm, in the frosty weather of January 26th 1848" (ix, 136). Cocks reported a number from Falmouth. In 1846, one was shot by Mr May on 29 October, a second seen by him "on the Pilot Boat Inn" on the 22nd November, and three shot "within a yard of each other" on 22 November 1847 (*RCPS*, 1849, p. 41 f.n.).

"This bird is not generally scatter'd along our Coast, & I believe not at all inward. But it prefers very circumscrib'd spots; passing from one of these places to another. It seems, in Wm Minard's opinion, that it is for the sake of a particular fly - apparently a kind of Ephemeron - but on examination the stomach contains little Beetles" (ix, 133-4). Ephemeron is any short-lived winged insect.

Bullmore's statement (1866, p.16) that they were found "every summer on the cliffs between Swanpool and Castle Head", Falmouth, may be an error. There is no proof that Black Redstarts bred in Cornwall in the 19th century, although in 1848 Couch thought they may have done so because the

"Black Start ... was seen in our hills in April & again at the end of July", though migrants are more likely (ix, 150). Birds did breed on the north coast near Crantock in 1929 and in the Perranporth area in the 1940s.

Note the records given under Common Redstart (**78**) that suggest Couch knew of the species in 1822.]

233 Grey-headed Wagtail [form of Yellow Wagtail *Motacilla flava*]

[Couch gave no details of the bird, a male with a slight mixture of olive green in the grey head feathers, obtained by D. W. Mitchell on the margins of a pool between Penzance and Marazion on 29 April 1839 (*MNH*, 1839, p. 467). Yellow Wagtails comprise a confusing group of subspecies.]

234 White Crossbill [Two-barred Crossbill *Loxia leucoptera*]

Reported by Mr Rodd.

[This species was formerly known as the White-winged Crossbill. Rodd's specimen was killed "at or near Lariggan {Madron} a few years since" and "was preserved in a very mutilated state as a supposed Chaffinch" (*RRIC*, 1840, p. 75). It is illustrated in J. T. Blight's *A Week at the Land's End* (1861, p. 31). Note also Couch's "Uncertain Species" (**54**) that must have been a Two-barred Crossbill.]

Two-barred Crossbill, after Blight

235 Rose-coloured Pastor [Rosy Starling *Sturnus roseus*]
Reported by Mr Rodd, and Mr Mitchell.
[E. H. Rodd was sent a specimen from Scilly in or before 1838 (*RRIC*, 1838, p. 40) and is illustrated by J.T. Blight (1861, p. 64). D.W. Mitchell saw an adult at the begionning of June 1839 at Gwithian (*MNH*, 1839, p. 467). F.V. Hill mentions one killed near Helston in 1830 (Johns, 1863 ed., *A week in The Lizard*, p. 325). The earliest record in Cornwall is of one shot by P. Pomery in his garden at Lostwithiel "some years since" (*MNH*, 1830, p. 176). Rodd examined two males and two females on 9 October 1855; three had been shot near Land's End and one "further east" (Couch, x, 274, copied from the *Zoologist*; see also *RCG*, 12 x). The following year, Richard Couch saw one caught near Penzance "within a day or two of 22 August" (x, 325). Rosy Starlings have been popular cage birds making it difficult to decide which are genuine migrants.]

Rosy Starling, after Blight

236 Dotterel [Eurasian Dotterel *Charadrius morinellus*]
[No information is given by Couch. Falmouth specimens from Maenporth, Bar Point and Gyllingvase, were examined by W. P. Cocks (Lithographed list, 1849; *TN*, 1851, p. 113), and another was obtained at Sancrccd in or before 1850 (E. H. Rodd, *Pz*, 1850, p. 417). It is a scarce annual migrant, mainly in the autumn.]

237 Spotted Redshank [*Tringa erythropus*]
Reported by Mr Rodd.
[This is Rodd's Dusky Sandpiper killed by Mr Pendaves "at the Land's End in the first week of September" 1840 (*RRIC*, 1840, p. 76). Couch included in his *Journal* a quote from the *West Briton* that one had been killed on Goonhilly Downs (x, 416), Bullmore (1866, p. 28) stating that it had been killed by James Clift of Grade on 3 December 1858. It is now a regular migrant and winter visitor in small numbers to Cornish estuaries.]

238 Wood Sandpiper [*Tringa glareola*]
Reported by Mr Rodd.
[Rodd reported that one had been killed, presumably in the Penzance area, in mid-December 1837. In 1840 he had another in June, while on 20 May a female was shot at Land's End, probably at

Mayon Pond or nearby freshwater. A further nine or ten were shot, seven of them in one day, in August the same year (Rodd, *RRIC*, 1840, pp. 75-76; *Pz*, 1850, p. 419; 1880, pp. 94-95, 193). The December record is unusual for this mainly autumn migrant, so when Clement Jackson told Couch on 25 December 1846 that he had sent a specimen he believed to be a Wood Sandpiper to Rodd, Couch thought it more probably a Green Sandpiper, "as I judge from the Season in which it was shot; the latter being more a winter bird" (ix 105-6).]

239 Pectoral Sandpiper [*Calidris melanotos*]

By Mr Mitchell.

[David William Mitchell (*c.*1813-1859), Secretary to the Zoological Society of London, lived in Penzance from 1832 until about 1842. He killed this American vagrant on the beach at Annet, Scilly, on 24 May 1840, and the following day saw another which mercifully escaped his gun. This was only the second British record and the first for Cornwall. Rodd published a detailed description of the bird in 1840 (*RRIC*, pp. 73-74), as did Yarrell (1843, Vol. II, 654-657). Cornish records are now more or less annual, mainly in the autumn.]

240 Eider Duck [Common Eider *Somateria mollissima*]

A female shot on the Looe River, Christmas 1839.

[Recorded by Couch (viii, 67) as shot on Christmas Eve. This is the first Cornish record of an uncommon passage migrant and winter visitor that has been reported annually since 1952.]

241 Long-tailed Duck [*Clangula hyemalis*]

A female taken at Penzance by Mr Mitchell. *West Briton*, April 1840.

[This bird was shot by David W. Mitchell at Marazion Marsh "on Friday last"(13 December) according to the *West Briton,* 20 xii 1839. J. C. Bellamy (1839, p. 217) noted that "Several specimens have been captured on the Tamar" without giving details. There appears to be no reference in the paper for April 1840.]

242 Iceland Gull [*Larus glaucoides*]

Obtained at Hayle in 1840.

[This is the only reference to this occurrence and, if correct, is the first for Cornwall. E. H. Rodd called it "rare" without further comment (*Pz*, 1850, p. 432). No other is reported until 1852 when an immature was killed by the Revd Jenkinson on Bryher, Scilly, in May (J. Clark & F. R. Rodd, 1906, p. 33).]

243 Wilson's Petrel [Wilson's Storm Petrel *Oceanites oceanicus*]

An account of the first specimen of this bird taken in the British islands, and which came into my possession, was communicated to the Linnean society; and is published in the 18th vol., of its Transactions, [1841] p.688[-690]. The specimen itself has been submitted to Mr Yarrell's inspection.

Wilson's Storm Petrel, after Yarrell

[Couch's account (viii, 7) of 24 August 1838 states that it "was taken dead in a field near Liskeard" and was set up by Clement Jackson. Couch sent the specimen to William Yarrell who figured it (1843, Vol. III, p. 516), but wrongly dated the find to November. The precise location of the find is not given by Couch, but was evidently between Polperro and Liskeard. In the *Trans. Linn. Soc.*, Couch states that about the middle of August the "Stormy Petrel abounded on the south coast of Cornwall, driven thither, it is probable, by a week's continuance of wind accompanied by rain; under which circumstances they are commonly found by thousands at a few miles from land, in the months of September and October. It is probable that the weather, as described above, had driven to us this rare stranger, the first of its species I believe on record as having occurred in Britain, which was found dead in a field at a few miles from Polperro, and was brought to me for examination. As our sailor boys were in possession of numerous living specimens of the Stormy Petrel, which are taken with great facility when the weather suits, I found no difficulty in instituting a comparative examination of these two species." Couch noted the larger size and heavier weight of Wilson's Petrel, the paler wing coverts and its longer legs "with a longitudinal stripe of sulphur-yellow, more golden at the borders, on the web between each toe". He conjectured that its stouter build made it more able than the Storm Petrel "to escape the violence of a storm; the reason, perhaps, why it does not more frequently come near our coasts".

Wilson's Storm Petrel breeds on islands off the Antarctic continent but is not uncommon well out to sea to the south and west of Britain between about June and October. By coincidence, it was in May 1838 that the bird artist John Gould set sail on HMS *Beagle* for Australia. "The early part of the passage was boistrous and adverse" and when the ship was "immediately off the Land's End, Wilson's Petrel was seen in abundance, and continued to accompany the ship throughout the Bay" (of Biscay) where they were delayed by eleven days, the little Storm Petrel being also seen, but in far less numbers: both species disappeared on approaching the latitude of Madeira" (*PZS*, 1839, p. 139). How close he really sailed to Land's End is not stated.]

Supplement, 1844, to the first two sections of Couch's *A Cornish Fauna*

244 Gyr Falcon [*Falco rusticolus*]

This Bird has hitherto occupied a place in the catalogue of the Cornish Fauna on the authority of a single specimen recorded by Borlase. Another instance of its occurrence is now to be added, on the authority of E. H. Rodd, Esq. in whose beautiful collection at Penzance the specimen is preserved [*J*, viii, 337].

[I have not found any reference to this species in Borlase (1758). Yarrell gives the same account (1843, Vol. I, p. 29), probably on the authority of Couch as he gives no full reference, adding that it was at Helston, perhaps confusing the bird mentioned below in Grylls' collection.

Rodd's specimen was an adult male with an injured wing captured on the banks of the River Lynher on 7 February 1834 (E. Moore, *MNH*, 1837). J. C. Bellamy (1839, p. 199) mistakenly said that this bird was captured at Morwell Rocks on the Devon side of the Tamar. It was kept alive by Pincombe, the Plymouth taxidermist, before it passed into Rodd's collection in June 1863. Rodd (1880, p. 7) only states, without date, that the specimen came from Port Eliot, St Germans, but as the estate borders the Lynher there can be little doubt that Moore's account is correct. This was not the first Cornish specimen. A tiercel shot at Gwavas, Grade, in 1830 was in the collection of Humphrey Grylls of Helston. The bird was later seen at Scorrier House by the Revd W. Willimott who described it as "the whitest I ever saw, living or dead", thus indicating the Greenland form (D'Urban & Mathew, 1892, p. 159).]

245 Ashcoloured Harrier [Montagu's Harrier *Circus pygargus*]

In a communication to the Royal Institution of Cornwall in 1840 (Report, p. 76), Mr Rodd has expressed his opinion that the specimen in the Museum in Truro supposed to represent this species, is erroneously marked; but he announces the possession of two specimens, a male and female, killed in Cornwall, and in his own collection.

[The adult male was killed in 1837 at Trelaske, Lewannick (E. Moore, *MNH*, 1837), and the female met the same fate near Trereife, Madron, in September or October 1840 (*RRIC*, 1840, p. 76). This has to be the harrier that Nicholas Hare described as one of the birds breeding on Bodmin Moor "every year" (*Pz*, 1848, pp.211-12). Rodd identified the specimen formerly in Truro Museum as an immature Marsh Harrier.]

246 Great Bustard [*Otis tarda*]

A specimen was shot on Goonhilly Downs, early in February 1843 [*J*, viii, 296]; and is now in the collection of E. H. Rodd, Esq. of Penzance. Of course it was a straggler from some eastward portion of the kingdom; and we may be permitted to regret that the rarity and value of the bird should deprive it of the chance of being propogated in a situation so well adapted for its residence.

[The bird had been seen for a few days in turnip fields on the Bonython estate, Cury, before being shot "within the last fortnight" (*WB*, 17 ii; Yarrell, 1843, Preface, pp. ix-x). The same bird was mentioned when in January 1854 another was "lately shot" near Polgooth Mine, St Austell, and sent to Mr P. Chapman the Falmouth taxidermist (x 183; *RCG*, 27 i; Rodd, 1864, p. 21). It was in the early 1830s that the Great Bustard ceased to breed in East Anglia.]

247 Red-legged Partridge [*Alectoris rufa*]

About the middle of September, 1842, a specimen of this bird was shot in the parish of Lanreath, and was sent to Mr C. Jackson of East Looe, to be preserved [*J*, viii, 280].

[This species was first introduced successfully into Britain in 1770. The first record of it in Cornwall is by Mr James of St Keverne who was told that Charles Rashleigh of St Austell "procured from abroad some of the red-legged, and turned them loose, and that they multiplied" (*IM*, 1808, p. 434). Birds are still introduced in some numbers, but breeding success is generally poor because they thrive best in warmer, drier summers.]

248 Garden Warbler [*Sylvia borin*]

Mr Rodd has added this species to the catalogue of Cornish birds; but its distribution seems to be local. It is found at Trebartha [North Hill].

[Rodd included this in his 1840 account (*RRIC*, 1840, p. 76) and told Couch about it in a letter the following year. The Garden Warbler remains a scarce breeding bird in east Cornwall. It was unknown to Couch in the Polperro area and his only other reference is to a bird shot on Scilly (ix, 224), one of several obtained "with other of our summer migrants ... in the autumn of 1849" (Rodd, *Pz*, 1850, p. 407).]

249 Richard's Pipit [*Anthus novaeseelandiae*]

This species of Lark has been usually regarded as rare; and it is not many years since I was present at a meeting of the Zoological Club of the Linnean Society when the first known specimen was produced for examination. But it is probably less rare than has been supposed; since four specimens were secured at one shot, in a field close to Penzance. It was noted that in their habits they were tame and void of suspicion.

Richard's Pipit from Redinnick, after Blight

[The first British migrant was taken alive "in the neighbourhood of London in October 1812" by N. A. Vigors who presented all his collection to the Zoological Society. Yarrell's illustration (1843, Vol. I, p. 398) was taken from this specimen. The four Cornish birds were shot in about mid-April 1843, though not quite as Couch thought. Two were dispatched with a single shot near Marazion, and two in Redinnick fields, Penzance, by W. A. Vingoe the Penzance taxidermist (A. Greenwood, *Z*, 1843). One that passed into Rodd's collection was illustrated by J. T. Blight (1861, p. 29). These were not the first because, in a letter to Couch dated 3 December 1841, Rodd said one had been captured "in a field near" Penzance (viii, 230-1). A few migrants are now reported annually, mainly in the autumn.]

250 Spoonbill [Eurasian Spoonbill *Platalea leucorodia*]

In the third week of October, 1843, nineteen of these birds were seen on the north coast of the county, near Newquay, and four of them killed: of which I examined a specimen [sent to Clement Jackson, *J*, viii, 285]. In the previous year, one was shot on the Goonhilly downs, and it is believed that these are not the only instances in which it has been taken.

A hen bird shot at Tregembris in Newlyn, is in the Museum, having been presented by Mr Robarts.

[The Spoonbill has long been a regular visitor, mostly immature birds in ones or twos at migration time with some remaining throughout the winter, though the records for 1843 are exceptional. The Newquay birds, "During the latter part of last week ... frequented the marshes of the Gannel River, and four of them were shot by different persons. One of them is in the possession of Mr N. Marshall of H. M. Customs, Newquay". Eleven flew over Hayle on 11 October and alighted on marshy ground near Gwithian where seven were killed at one shot by Richard Hocking (*WB* and *RCG*, 20 xi). J. S. Courtney (1845, p. 30) wrote that a flock was seen on the beach between Penzance and Marazion, and many were afterwards killed "near Perranporth".

The Tregembris bird, presented to Truro Museum by John Robarts, was shot in October 1843 (*RRIC*, 1843, p. 20), while one was killed on Goonhilly Downs on 4 November 1842 "and now in the possession of Mr Chapman of Falmouth" (viii, 285; *Falmouth Packet*, 11 xi).

Such a large bird would easily attract attention, so 19th century records are not very rare. Bellamy (1839, p. 210) recorded one shot on the Tamar in December 1835, and another (on the Tamar?) in December 1838, while Couch noted birds shot on the Lynher on 26 April 1852 and at the end of December 1858, where another had been shot "3 years ago by the same person, Mr Spencer" (x, 60, 417). An immature was shot in St Buryan parish on 8 October 1845 (ix, 59; *RCG*, 17 x; *Pz*, 1846, p. 44).]

Birds noted by Couch in his *Natural History Journal* but not published by him.
They are appended here in chronological order of occurrence.

251 Common Pheasant [*Phasanius colchicus*]

[1833. In common with most bird-watchers, Couch largely ignored this naturalized bird, but on 18 November 1833 he recorded that one shot at Trelawne Wood, Pelynt, "had about half a pint of Acorns in its crop, most of which had grown & in some the radicle was sprouted to the length of 1 inch" (vi, 73). Acorns, hazel-nuts and beechmast are among its most common vegetable food.]

252 Nightingale [Common Nightingale *Luscinia megarhynchos*]

[1838. This undistinguished looking skulking summer visitor is occasionally reported as a passage migrant in Cornwall and almost annually on Scilly. Birds remained throughout the summer in 1978 and 1989, and a nest near Lawhitton church was robbed in 1940. Early records are suspect and E. H. Rodd (1880) called it "unknown in Cornwall". Couch did not publish any records, presumably doubting the following account (vii, 283-4). Clement Jackson received from Mr R. Lakes of St Austell a specimen with a note dated 30 April 1838, "& the Bird must have been alive within a day or two of that date. No information is given as to whether it had been {in} Captivity; but in the Note Mr L. expresses doubt what the Bird really is; & the feathers & feet are clean as if it had been wild". Summer residents do arrive from mid-April and the record may be correct, bearing in mind an occurrence in the previous year that Couch ignored, even though it was published by his friend C. W. Peach. "In the summer of 1837, a nightingale visited the groves in the vicinity of Caerhayes, and the neighbourhood of Tregavarris in Goran; I heard her sing *many times*, at *different hours*, as her song reminded me of 'Auld lang syne' in my nocturnal rounds; I frequently rode in the direction of Caerhayes, to live as it were my early days over again, my native village in Northamptonshire being famed for nightingales; she was heard by many, some of the men belonging to the Preventive Service who also had in their youth been accustomed to the song of the nightingale, were like myself delighted to hear the warbling of their nocturnal friend; she remained nearly through the summer, and was frequently seen by the gamekeeper, he tried to shoot her, and said she was a small brown bird; she has not been heard there since" (*RRIC*, 1841, p. 30).

It was also "in the neighbourhood" of St Austell that "different persons" heard the "sweet notes of the nightingale" during the last fortnight in June 1855 (*WB*, 29 vi). Not all songs at the appropriate time of year must of necessity be attributed to other more common songbirds.]

253 Egyptian Goose [*Alopochen aegyptiacus*]

(See also under **220** Spur-winged Goose)

[1841. Three Egyptian Geese killed "in west Cornwall" in December (ix, 158) were shot on Monday the 27th at "the fowling pond" at Skewjack, Sennen, by James Trembath, jun." (*WB*, 31 xii), apparently the first for Cornwall. Another was shot "last week" near Gunwalloe and was purchased by Frederick V. Hill of Helston (*WB* & *RCG*, 24 xi 1848), and another shot at Helford by Mr. Veale, ferryman, in autumn 1849 (W.P. Cocks, *TN*, 1851, p. 138). Couch noted in 1853 that this species had been kept on the pool at Tresco, Scilly, "for many years; & they are at liberty to fly away if they choose it" (x, 160).]

254 Black-winged Stilt [*Himantopus himantopus*]

[1844. Writing late in the following year, Couch noted "Himantopus - Stilt plover - kill'd at Falmouth a year & half since, & one seen at Swanpool in 1844 - on the authority of Mr Tresidder" (ix, 57). Both probably refer to the same bird that W. P. Cocks reported, without date, shot at Swanpool by Mr J. Genn, Silversmith, and not in 1851 as stated elsewhere (*RCPS*, 1849, p. 45).]

255 Red-crested Pochard [*Netta rufina*]

[1845. "Fuligula rufa (*sic*) kill'd & brought to Falmouth Market" (ix, 10). It was shot at Swanpool in February and was sold for sixpence (*RCPS*, 1849, p. 47). This is the first for Cornwall, but as with most records of this species, it is rarely possible to know if they are wild or escaped from captivity.]

256 Firecrest [*Regulus ignicapillus*]

[1845. Couch noted under Goldcrest in his 1838 account that "The Fire Crested Wren, which has been confounded with this, has been reported to me, but I have not examined a Cornish specimen". The first fully authenticated Cornish records were in 1845. On 1 March the gardener at Trevince, Gwennap, found two huddled together on the snow-covered path, and another was reported by Vingoe on the 6th "in the Minney", Penzance, "busying about for insects" (*WB*, 21 iii; *Z*, 1845, pp. 942, 1023). The Trevince birds, seen in October by Couch who drew the head of the male (ix, 10), had passed to Nicholas Tresidder of Falmouth who reported that another had been shot by his brother near Falmouth "twelve years ago" (*WB*, 4 iv 1845), perhaps the one reported to Couch in his 1838 account. Couch also noted (ix, 105) that the *West Briton* of 1 January reported a pair shot by Mr Passmore near Truro in the middle of December 1846. I can find no such report (nor in *RCG*), but a male and female were shot by Mr Passmore the taxidermist on 23 January 1852 near Carvedras, Truro, and "another in the parish of St Clement" in April (*WB*, 30 i and 23 iv), Couch inferred "from this and former instances that the Birds make the west of our County their winter retreat & that the male & female do not separate" (x, 39-40).

Firecrests are now regular winter visitors. Their breeding range expanded into southern England in 1962 and in recent years nesting has been suspected in Devon, though not yet in Cornwall.]

257 Buff-breasted Sandpiper [*Tryngites subruficollis*]

[1846. One killed by Lady Carrington's servant on the sands between Penzance and Marazion on 3 September (ix 97; *Pz*, 1846, p. 87 says 1845 in error; Rodd, 1880, p. 196). Charlotte Carrington (1770-23 April 1849) died in Bath but spent much time at The Orchard, Penzance. This is the first Cornish example of a species that is now reported more or less annually in Cornwall and Scilly where it is more easily seen than in its breeding grounds in the American Arctic. Fifteen were on St Mary's airfield on 8 September 1977.]

258 White-rumped Sandpiper [*Calidris fuscicollis*]

[1846. Couch reported two under the old scientific name of *Tringa schinzii* shot on the Hayle estuary (ix, 105). This north American vagrant has been called both Schinz's and Bonaparte's Sandpiper. The two, a male and female, were shot on 13 October, the first for Cornwall, and passed into E. H. Rodd's collection (Rodd, 1880, pp. 105, 197-8).]

259 Crested Lark [*Galerida cristata*]

[1846. Two males, the first for Cornwall, were shot on 9 September by W. H. Vingoe who spotted them on a Cornish hedge by the roadside at Marazion Green, the area between Marazion Marsh and the foreshore. He was attracted to them "by the melodious quality of their song" (ix, 97; *Pz*, 1846, p. 89 says 1845 in error; *Z*, 1846, p. 1497). Another set up by Vingoe was shot in the same area by J. N. R. Millet on or before 25 October 1850 (*Z*, 1850, p. 3033). Although a widespread species on the Continent, it remains a rare British vagrant.]

260 Ivory Gull [*Pagophila eburnea*]

[1847. This is the rarest of the Arctic white gulls recorded in Britain. The first Cornish example, noted by Couch without details (ix, 107), was an immature with sparse "well defined dusky brown spots", seen for a few days about the Battery Rocks, Penzance, until it was shot on 15 February by

Michael Roberts. It may have been the same bird seen on Friday the 13th at Bar Point, Falmouth, by W. P. Cocks and Mr Spence (*Z*, 1847, p. 1699; *RCPS*, 1847, p. 48; Rodd, 1880, p.170). A second was seen at Falmouth about the same date and ultimately shot near Quilquay [Kiln Quay, Flushing, Mylor] by Mr Olive, the watchmaker; it was preserved by Mr Chapman who sold it "to a commercial traveller of Bath" (Bullmore, 1866, p. 43, but wrongly gives the year as 1837).]

261 Scops-eared Owl [Eurasian Scops Owl *Otus scops*]

Eurasian Scops Owl from Gould's Birds of Great Britain,
by kind permission of the Natural History Museum, London.

[1847. This, the smallest owl on the British list, is a rare visitor between April and September. It was seen more frequently in the 19th century than subsequently. E. H. Rodd reported in a letter to the

Zoologist (1847, p. 1773) that he received on Monday 12 April one that had been caught in an exhuasted state, but in perfect condition, on Tresco, Scilly, "in the past week in the grounds of Mr Smith, the lord-proprietor in the island". It proved to be a male and was subsequently loaned to John Gould who figured it in colour in Vol. 1, Plate 33, of his *Birds of Great Britain* (1862-73). It is the greyer of two birds shown, the one with a Death's-head Hawk-moth (*Acherontia atropos*) in its beak. Insects are its main diet. Rodd was mistaken, however, when he said (1880, p.260) that grey birds were males and the rufous-toned females; the sexes are similar though variable in colour. J. Clark & F. R. Rodd (*Z*, 1906) said the bird was captured by Christian Holliday, but wrongly gave the date of capture as 13 April. After E. H. Rodd's death, the bird graced his nephew's collection at Trebartha Hall, North Hill, but the specimen no longer exists.]

262 White Stork [*Ciconia ciconia*]

[1848. Couch's note (ix, 145) refers to an adult shot by the servant of James Trembath on Mayon Pond, Sennen, on 13 May, "having flown in from seawards" (*RCG*, 19 v; R. Q. Couch MS). This is the first Cornish record of what remains a rare vagrant.]

263 Black Tern [*Childonias niger*]

[1848. September, "A Black Tern shot on a Moor at Deep Hatches {Altarnun} ... in the early part of this month, reported in the Penzance Gazette" of 20 October (ix, 152). An earlier note in the *Penzance Journal* of the 13th, dates it to "last week", so on or before the 9th. W. P. Cocks (annotated copy of Couch's *A Cornish Fauna*) noted six shot at Swanpool, Falmouth, in October 1849. It has always been a regular autumn migrant, though rarely seen in its full black plumage, as noted by E. H. Rodd in a specimen from Penzance in April 1851 (*RRIC*, 1851, p. 52). On 22 September 1852, Couch described in detail a bird he took to be an immature Black Tern, "although there is some doubt in assigning it", but did not say from where he had obtained it (x, 86). His description certainly fits this species.]

264 Whiskered Tern [*Chlidonias hybridus*]

[1851. This is among new birds noted by Couch without details (x, 33). It was an immature shot by Augustus Pechell at Tresco Pool, Scilly, on 2 August 1851 (some accounts say "in September") and passed into E. H. Rodd's collection (*Pz*, 1852, pp. 66-7, 1864, p. 37; Clark & Rodd, 1906, p. 31 state 2 August).]

265 Sabine's Gull [*Larus sabini*]

[1851. Couch noted (*J*, x, 32) from the *Cornish Telegraph* of 3 October 1851 that one had been shot on the 2nd by Michael Roberts of Penzance near the pier, a "beautiful specimen of Sabine's Xeme", but there was an earlier occurrence of this rare Arctic gull. R. Q. Couch (MS.) said a young specimen was shot in Falmouth harbour in 1822, the initials "C.J." presumably meaning Clement Jackson. If true, it is contemporary with the first British specimen shot in Belfast Bay in September that year, but it is possible that Richard Couch re-identified the 1824 Little Gull that his father illustrated (see **190**) but got the date wrong. There is no record of Jackson killing a supposed Little Gull in 1822 in Falmouth or elsewhere. Sabine's Gull was readily mistaken for the Little Gull because Selby (*Illustrations of British Ornithology*, 1821-34) erroneously credited the Little Gull with having a pronounced forked tail. E. H. Rodd reported a Sabine's Gull before 1850 (*Pz*, 1850, p.431) without further details but which again could refer to the 1824 bird.]

266 Pomarine Skua [*Stercorarius pomarinus*]

Pomarine Skua, after Eyton

[1851. Among the birds new to Cornwall, Couch notes this species without details, but adds "this I have possessed". The 1851 bird was an adult taken in "the immediate neighbourhood of Penzance", but the exact date is not recorded (Rodd, *RRIC*, 1851, p. 52). Most are reported in September and October.

The bird Couch possessed was a skua taken with a line off Polperro in September 1846. He thought it was an Arctic Skua, but Clement Jackson believed it to be a Pomarine "on the authority of

Eyton" (1836, p. 53), though Eyton's illustration is not good. Yarrell figured an immature (1843, Vol. III, p. 485), only the 4th edition (1882-4, Vol.III, p. 688) also showing an adult and noting the central tail feathers extending "four inches beyond the others". Couch later examined it again "in comparison with Specimens of the other Species" and Yarrell's description and was "compelled to admit" that Jackson was right. Unfortunately, he did not fully describe it. The bill was "thicker and stronger" than the Arctic's, its wingspan was four feet and its length just under two feet with the middle tail feathers extending 4 inches beyond the others, measurement which more or less fit the Pomarine (ix, 97, 99, 108-9).]

267 Least Sandpiper [*Calidris minutilla*]

[1853. This vary rare vagrant, originally called an American Stint, was first recorded in Britain when one was shot "in Mount's Bay", probably at or near Marazion Marsh on 10 October by W. S. Vingoe who found it "alone on a piece of wet grass land adjoining the sea-shore, and rose silently" (x, 209; Rodd, 1880, p. 108). No other was reported in Cornwall until 1890, killed by Mr A. McFadyean (*Pz*, 1890-91, p. 272), the bird seen by James Clark in 1902, "killed by a fisherman near Mousehole in September 1890", incorrectly labelled as a Little Stint in the collection of W. E. Baily of Paul (*Z*, 1907).]

268 Short-toed Lark [Greater Short-toed Lark *Calandrella brachydactyla*]

[1854. Couch's note (x, 209) is taken from the *Zoologist* for October. The bird was shot by Augustus Pechell at Skirt Point, Tresco, on 23 September, where it had been feeding on grasses growing in the sand a few yards from the beach (Rodd, 1864, p. 15). No other local example was recorded until one frequented the shoreline at Porth Mellon, St Mary's, Scilly, from 26 to 28 October 1954.]

269 Long-billed Dowitcher [*Limnodromus scolopaceus*]

Dowitcher sp., after Blight

[1857. The American ornithologist F. A. Pitelka confirmed in 1950 that there are two distinct species of dowitcher. It is now known that the Long-billed Dowitcher is a regular vagrant to Britain. It is rarely possible to assign early records or, indeed, many recent sightings, to this or to the very similar Short-billed (*L. griseus*). The first Cornish vagrant, which passed into E. H. Rodd's collection, was shot by Augustus Pechell on the Higher Moors, St Mary's, Scilly, on 3 October 1857 (*RCG*, 9 x; *RRIC*, 1857, p. 18). Couch referred to it as a Brown Snipe (x, 381), and it is figured by J. T. Blight as a "Brown Longbeaked Snipe" (1861, p. 169). Its bill was 2 inches long, suggesting a Long-billed, but bill measurements of the two species overlap and the rest of the description is not diagnostic. The call notes are distinctive, but Pechell's bird did not utter a sound.]

270 Spotted Eagle [Greater Spotted Eagle *Aquila clanga*]

[1860. The bird noted by Couch as having been killed "in a covert under Kilmar" (x, 500) was a first year male shot by F. R. Rodd's steward H. Couch on 4 December 1860 at Hawk's Wood, North Hill. The yellow spotting is lost in adulthood. "It was observed first in a tree, and on the approach of the shooting party, instead of soaring, the bird shuffled down the tree and scrambled under some rocks ... one of the wings was broken, but whether shot or otherwise I cannot exactly determine ... the body, wings, and every part of the body exhibited the most perfect form, but probably some injury at some time prevented the bird from taking flight" (*RRIC*, 1861, pp. 40-42; *RCG*, 14 xii). It passed into E. H. Rodd's collection and was seen by the famous ornithologist H. E. Dresser in 1885 when the bird had passed to F. R. Rodd of Trebartha Hall.

This was the first confirmed Spotted Eagle reported in England, though one may well have been shot on Lundy, Devon, in the winter of 1858; the bird rolled over the cliff, could not be recovered and was identified by a few remaining spotted feathers (D'Urban & Mathew, 1892, p. 149). By a strange coincidence, the second confirmed English specimen, noted by Couch without details (x, 500), also came from Cornwall. This was another young male shot by James Jones on 29 October 1861 at Trevedras farm, St Mawgan-in-Pydar. He first noted it hovering at a great height "and thought it appeared to be coming down". After dinner "he took his gun with him to the field, and on looking about, he saw the bird at work on a carcase of a dead horse, not far off; he made towards it under cover of a hedge, and succeeded in killing it" (*RCG*, 1 xi). It was reported here as a Golden eagle, but corrected the following week "by an eminent ornithologist" (*RCG*, 8 xi). The bird was sent to the Penzance taxidermist W. H. Vingoe who found it "in low condition" (*RRIC*, 1862, pp. 5, 41-42; Rodd, 1880, p. 227, wrongly stated that it was shot in November). It was presented by the landowner, E. Brydges Willyams, to the Royal Institution of Cornwall, Truro, where it remains in excellent plumage.]

Spotted Eagle from St. Mawgan-in-Pydar (author's photograph).

271 Red-breasted Flycatcher [*Ficedula parva*]

1863. "I read in the Cornwall Gazette for Feby 6 that an example ... was shot in this County on Carythenack [*sic*] House; a female. Dr J. E. Gray had given its name - it must have been shot a short time since. It is the first time of its being known in Britain" [*J*, xi, 38].

[Horace Copeland of Carwythenack, Constantine, shot the bird on 24 January, a very unusual date as most are now recorded in autumn. It had been seen about for several days, a dead holly tree near the house being its favourite perch. The head was eaten by mice, but sufficent remained for it to be identified some time later as a female by the distinguished naturalist John Gould who chanced to be in Falmouth the very day it was shot and who sent it to Dr Gray at the British Museum. A second bird, seen in a plantation about 400 yards away, fortunately escaped (*RRIC*, 1863, pp. 36-7). An immature male was shot by Augustus Pechell in Tresco Abbey gardens on 16 October the same year (*Z*, October 1863, *RRIC*, 1864, p. 50), while another was shot on Tresco on 5 November 1865 after Pechell and the Revd Jenkinson had watched it "busily engaged in capturing flies" (*Z*, November 1866; Rodd 1880, p. 28). No other was recorded in Cornwall until 1944 when one was seen on Morvah Hill on 30 September.]

272 Red-legged Falcon [Red-footed Falcon *Falco vespertinus*]
1867. "My friend, Mr Cocks of Falmouth informs me that an example of the Redlegged Falcon - Falco Rufipes, was shot near Helston a few days before 20 Novr, & is in possession of Mr Bullmore - Surgeon, of Helston" [*J*, xii, 80].
[The bird was shot at Nansloe, Wendron (*RCG*, 5 xii). This was only the second recorded Cornish occurrence of this uncommon migrant. W. P. Cocks flushed one from "Mr Jago's furze patch stone quarry" at Budock on 6 February 1851. "After hawking close to the ground in Mr Selly's field for nearly ten minutes, it mounted high and made off for the wood at Trefusis, about half-a-mile from the furze brake" (*TN*, 1851, p. 163; Bullmore 1866, p. 9).]

BIBLIOGRAPHY
Other works are noted in full in the text.

BELLAMY, J. C., 1839, *The Natural History of South Devon*, Plymouth & London.

BEWICK, T., 1826 (6th ed.), *A History of British Birds*, 2 vols., Newcastle. The work first appeared in 1797, the 1826 edition containing new material.

BLIGHT, J. T., 1861, *A Week at the Land's End*, Truro and London.

BORLASE, William, 1758, *The Natural History of Cornwall*, Oxford. Borlase's "Additions" were published by the Royal Institution of Cornwall, *JRIC*, 1864-1866.

BULLMORE, W. K., 1866, "Cornish Fauna", *RCPS*, "Birds" pp. 7-45. This deals mainly with the Falmouth area and covers "the last six years". It was issued separately in the following year.

CAREW, Richard, 1602, *The Survey of Cornwall*. The edition used is F. E. Halliday, 1953, *Richard Carew of Antony*, London.

CLARK, J., 1906, "Birds" in *The Victoria County History, Cornwall*, Vol. 1, London. (This is an expanded account of "The Birds of Cornwall", 1902, *JRIC*, 179-228.

CLARK, J., 1907, "Recent Occurrences of Rare Birds in Cornwall", *Zoologist* (also as offprint, 7 pages).

CLARK, J., 1908, "Bird Migration in Cornwall", *JRIC*, pp. 274-293.

CLARK, J. & RODD, F. R., 1906, "The Birds of Scilly", *Zoologist* (July-September, and reprinted separately, 35 pages).

COUCH, J., 1822, "Of the Migratory Birds of the west of England", *The Imperial Magazine*.

COUCH, J., JACKSON, C. & LAKES, M., 1830, "Rare or uncommon Birds observed in Cornwall, particularly in the southern parts of the county", *MNH*, Vol. 3, 175-177.

COUCH, J., 1838, *A Cornish Fauna*, Part 1, Royal Institution of Cornwall, Truro (Birds pp. 10-30). An *Appendix* to Part 2 (1841) is a modified report presented to the Meeting of the British Association for Science at Plymouth in 1841 (Birds pp. 69-70).
A *Supplement* (1844) to parts 1 and 2 (Birds pp.145-148).

COUCH, J., 1847, *Illustrations of Instinct deduced from the habits of British Animals*, London.

COUCH, R., Q., (MS.), Annotations in his copy of J. Couch's 1838 *A Cornish Fauna* at the R.I.C., Truro.

COURTNEY, J. S., 1845, *A Guide to Penzance and its Neighbourhood, Including the Islands of Scilly*, London & Penzance. An account of birds appears on pp. 25-35.

D'URBAN, W. S. & MATHEW, M. A., 1892, *The Birds of Devon*, London. (2nd edition in 1895 with a Supplement.) Contains much data on Cornwall.

EDMONDS, R., 1862, *The Land's End District*, London and Penzance.

EYTON, T. C., 1836, *A History of the Rarer British Birds*, London.

FLEMING, J., 1828, *A History of British Animals*, Edinburgh.

FOX, G. T., 1827, *Synopsis of the Newcastle Museum*, Newcastle. Pages 252-255 refer to bird specimens and notes from Henry Mewburn (1780-1834), then of St Germans, Cornwall.

GILBERT, C. S., 1817, *An Historical Survey of the County of Cornwall*, Vol. 1, London and Plymouth Dock. Vol. 2 was published in 1820.

GREGORY, G, 1806 (2nd ed. 1813), *A Dictionary of Arts and Sciences*, 2 vols., Thomas Tagg, London. Couch used the 2nd edition.

HARE, N., 1846, "Liskeard Ornithology", *RCPS*, pp. 25-35.

JAMES, S., of St. Keverne 1808-1810, "The Literary Repository of Cornwall and Devon", *The Monthly Magazine*, Birds 1808, pp. 433-435; 1809, pp. 527-528. Published anonymously.

LEVER, C., 1977, *The Naturalized Animals of the British Isles*, London.

MONTAGU, G., 1802, *Ornithological Dictionary of British Birds*, London. A *Supplement* was added in 1813. There are subsequent editions, the 2nd by James Rennie, 1831, London.

MOORE, E, 1830, "On the ornithology of South Devon", *TPI*, pp.289-352.

RAY, J., 1678, *The Ornithology of Francis Willughby of Middleton in the County of Warwick*, London. A facsimile edition was published in 1972, Newport Pagnell.

RODD, E. H., 1864, *A List of British Birds, as a Guide to the Ornithology of Cornwall, especially in the Land's End District*, London and Penzance (a rare 2nd edition appeared in 1869. Rodd's first list was published in *Pz*, 1850, pp. 400-434).

RODD, E.H., 1880, *The Birds of Cornwall and the Scilly Isles* (edited after his death by J. E. Harting), London.

SARGEANT, T. (Ed.), 1726, *The Works of Walter Moyle, Esq.; None of which were ever before published*, 2 vols, London. Moyle, born in 1672, died in 1721.

YARRELL, W., 1843, *A History of British Birds*, 3 vols, London. The revised, enlarged 4th ed., 1871-74, was edited by Alfred Newton (vols. I and II) and James Saunders (vols. III and IV).

INDEX

Index to current English names of species. Numbers are those given to the species and not to pages. Main references are in bold type.

Accentor, Hedge (Dunnock) 34, **81**

Auk, Little **174**

Avocet, Pied **147**

Bee-eater, European **31**

Bittern, Great **155**

       Little **152**

Blackbird, Common **43**, 45

Blackcap **61**

Bluethroat **222**

Brambling **57**

Bullfinch, Common **51**, 55

Bunting, Cirl **64**

       Corn **62**

       Ortolan **66**

       Reed **65**

       Snow **67**

Bustard, Great **246**

       Little **118**

Buzzard, Common 1, **4**

      see also Honey-buzzard

Chaffinch 41, 46, **56**, 114

Chiffchaff, Common 87, **88**, 100

Chough, Red-billed 24, **25**

Coot, Common 116, **117**

Cormorant, Great 174, **175**

Crake, Corn **112**

       Little **115**

       Spotted **113**

Crane, Common...	**149**
Crossbill, Common...	**52**
Two-barred..	**54, 234**
Crow, Carrion..	**21**
Hooded...	**22**
Cuckoo, Common..	**34**, 100
Yellow-billed...	**35**
Curlew, Common...	**145**, 146
Dipper, White-throated...	32, **33**
Diver, Black-throated...	165, 166
Great Northern...	**164, 166**
Red-throated...	**165, 170**
Dotterel, Eurasian..	**236**
Dove, European Turtle...	**107**
Dowitcher, Long-billed..	**269**
Short-billed..	269
Duck, Long-tailed..	**241**
Tufted..	**218**
Dunlin...	**130**, 131, 133
Dunnock, see Accentor, Hedge.	
Eagle, Golden...	1
Greater Spotted..	270
Eider, Common..	**240**
Egret, Little...	**154**, 157
Falcon, Gyr..	244
Peregrine..	**3**
Red-footed..	**272**
Fieldfare...	41, **42**, 46
Firecrest..	**256**
Flycatcher, Pied..	91
Red-breasted..	**271**

Spotted..**91**
Fulmar, Northern..**180**

Gadwall..**213**
Gannet, Northern..**177**
Garganey..**227**
Godwit, Bar-tailed..**141, 148**
    Black-tailed.. 141
Goldcrest...**89**, 256
Goldeneye, Common..**216, 217**
Goldfinch, European...**55**
Goosander...**195, 196**, 197
Goose, Bean..**203**
    Brent...**204**
    Canada..**200**
    Egyptian.. 220, **253**
    Greater White-fronted..................................**202**
    Greylag..**201**
    Spur-winged...**220**
Grebe, Black-necked..**161**
    Great Crested...**158**
    Little..**163**
    Red-necked..**159**
    Slavonian..160, 161, **162**
Greenfinch, European...53
Greenshank, Common..**143**
Grouse, Black..**111**
Guillemot, Common..**167, 168**
    Black...**169**
Gull, Black-headed...**191**, 192
    Common (see Mew)
    Glaucous...**228**
    Great Black-backed **186**, 188
    Herring..**188**, 189

Iceland	**242**
Ivory	**260**
Laughing	191
Lesser Black-backed	**187**, 188
Little	**190**, 265
Mediterranean	191
Mew or Common	188, **189**, 191
Sabine's	190, **265**

Harrier, Eurasian Marsh ... **5**, 245
    Hen ... **5**, **8**, 9
    Montagu's ... **9, 245**
Hawfinch ... **50**
Heron, Black-crowned Night ... **226**
    Grey ... **150**
    Purple ... **151**
    Squacco ... 154, **157**
Honey-buzzard, European ... **229**
Hoopoe ... **30**

Ibis, Glossy ... **156**

Jackdaw, Eurasian ... 23, **24**, 25
Jay, Eurasian ... **27**

Kingfisher, Common ... **32**
Kite, Red ... **2**
Kestrel, Common ... 6, **10**
Kittiwake, Black-legged ... 190, 191, **192**
Knot, Red ... **125, 127**, 132

Lapwing, Northern ... **121**
Lark, Crested ... **259**
    Greater Short-toed ... **268**

Sky	46, **68**
Wood	68, **69**
Linnet, Common	19, 46, 57, **58**, 59
Magpie, Black-billed	**26**
Mallard	**207**
Martin, House	60, 99, **100**
Sand	**101**
Merganser, Red-breasted	**196, 197**
Merlin	**11**
Moorhen, Common	**116**
Nightjar, European	**103**
Nightingale	69, 84, **252**
Nutcracker, Spotted	**28**
Nuthatch, Wood	**39**
Oriole, Eurasian Golden	**47**
Osprey	**7**
Ouzel, Ring	**44**
Owl, Barn	**15**
Eurasian Scops	**261**
Long-eared	**12**
Northern Hawk	**13**
Short-eared	12, **14**
Snowy	**230**
Tawny	**16, 17**
Oystercatcher, Eurasian	**136**
Partridge, Grey	**109**
Red-legged	**247**
Petrel (see under Storm-petrel)	
Phalarope, Grey	**137**
Red-necked	137

Pheasant, Common	111, **251**
Pigeon, Common Wood	**105**, 106, 108
Rock	**106**
Stock	106, **108**
Pintail, Northern	**215**
Pipit, Meadow	34, 70, **71**
Richard's	**249**
Rock	34, **70**, 71
Tree	**72**
Plover, European Golden	**120**, 123
Great Ringed	**122**
Grey	**123**
Pochard, Common	203, **214**
Red-crested	**255**
Puffin, Atlantic	169, **173**
Quail, Common	109, **110**
Rail, Water	**114**
Raven, Common	**20**, 186
Razorbill	167, 168, **171, 172**
Redpoll, Lesser	59
Redshank, Common	**144**
Spotted	**237**
Redstart, Black	78, **80, 232**
Common	**78**
Redwing	43, 45, **46**, 155
Robin, European	55, 74, **77**
Roller, European	**29**
Rook	3, 21, **23**, 24, 49
Ruff	**126**
Sanderling	**124**
Sandpiper, Buff-breasted	**257**

Common	**129**, 134
Curlew	**131**, 185
Green	**128**, 238
Least	**267**
Pectoral	**239**
Purple	**132**
White-rumped	**258**
Wood	**238**
Scaup, Greater	**208**
Scoter, Black	**205**
Surf	**206**
Shag, European	21, 175, **176**
Shearwater, Great	**179**
Manx	**179**
Sooty	**179**, 180
Shelduck, Common	**209**
Shoveler, Northern	**210, 211**
Shrike, Great Grey	**18**, 231
Red-backed	**19**
Woodchat	**231**
Siskin, Eurasian	**225**
Skua, Arctic	**193**
Great	**194**
Long-tailed	**193**
Pomarine	**266**
Smew	**198**
Snipe, Common	**139**, 155
Great	**142**
Jack	**140**
Sparrow, House	**60**, 100
Sparrowhawk, Eurasian	**6**
Spoonbill, Eurasian	**250**
Starling, Common	46, **49**
Rosy	**235**

Stilt, Black-winged..**254**
Stint, American (see Sandpiper, Least)
    Little...**133**, 134
    Temminck's..**134**
Stonechat...70, **83**
Stone-curlew...**119**
Stork, Black...**153**
    White..**262**
Storm-petrel, European...**178**, 243
    Leach's...**181**
    Wilson's..178, **243**
Swallow, Barn..**99**, 100
Swan, Bewick's (see Tundra)
    Black..**221**
    Tundra...**199**
    Whooper..**199**
Swift, Alpine..**104**
    Common...**102**

Teal, Common..**219**
Tern, Arctic..182
    Black..**263**
    Common...**182**
    Little..**183**
    Roseate...**185**
    Sandwich..**184**, 185
    Whiskered..**264**
Thrush, Mistle...**41**, 46, 77
    Song..43, **45**, 77
Tit, Bearded...**98**
    Blue...93, **94**
    Coal...**95**
    Great...92, **93**, 94
    Long-tailed...**96**

Marsh	95, **97**
Willow	97
Treecreeper, Eurasian	**92**
Turnstone, Ruddy	120, **135**
Wagtail, Grey	**75**, 76
Grey-headed (see Yellow)	
Pied/White	**74**
Yellow	75, **76**, **233**
Warbler, Common Grasshopper	**73**
Dartford	**79**
Garden	**248**
Reed	84
Sedge	81, **84**
Willow	86, **87**
Wood	**86**
Waxwing, Bohemian	**48**
Wheatear, Northern	10, 32, 64, **82**, 100
Whimbrel	**146**
Whinchat	**224**
Whitethroat, Common	**85**, 92
Lesser	**223**
Wigeon, Eurasian	**212**
Woodcock, Eurasian	68, 112, **138**
Woodpecker, Great Spotted	**37**
Green	**36**, 38, 39
Lesser Spotted	**38**
Wren, Winter	77, **90**
Wryneck, Eurasian	**40**
Yellowhammer	**63**